# Meet My Friend David

# Meet My Friend

# David

Jane McWhorter

QUALITY PUBLICATIONS
P.O. BOX 7385
FT. WORTH, TX 76111

© Jane McWhorter 1982

ISBN: 0-89137-420-5

Dedicated with love to my daddy

# Introduction

David has always fascinated me. On several different occasions I've spent months at a time trying to unravel the mysteries of this great man.

On trips to Israel I've visited what I was told is the tomb of David in the Mount Zion section of Jerusalem. Without a doubt, this part of modern Jerusalem was David's entire Jerusalem. Whether David's body was buried at this particular spot is of no real consequence. The Jews, however, honor the supposed entombment of their beloved leader with great reverence and awe. Candles burn, religious leaders chant prayers, and male visitors are not allowed to enter with uncovered heads. As we walked through this stone shrine, I thought a great deal about David. It really does not matter where his bones have been buried. He died about three thousand years ago and his body has long since decayed. But David has a message, both in his written word and in his life, that still echoes through the ages. It is a message of hope and encouragement for all of us. David was far from perfect. He committed many wrongs, some of them much worse than most of us will ever commit. Yet this second king of Israel is referred to as a man after God's own heart (1 Samuel 13:14). What was there about David's character, vile and wicked in so many ways, that pleased God? Solving this mystery will be the underlying theme of the entire study.

I believe we can make David step out of the pages of the Scriptures and truly seem alive to you. There were a lot of high points, or mountain peaks, in the life of David. These are the things we usually think about when we mention his name. There were also many little, uneventful, often unnoticed happenings which truly tell us what David was really like. We'll view the mountain peaks of this king's life, but we'll also zoom in for a closer look at some of the valleys with their seldom noticed events.

There was a time when some of David's words, planted deeply in my subconscious mind, were of great comfort and strength to me when my conscious mind was not always in full touch with reality. Those implanted words sustained me when I needed them most. This study is my way of thanking God for one of His most beloved inspired writers.

Meet my friend David. I think you'll enjoy knowing him better.

Jane

# The Development of a Person after God's Own Heart

"And he shall be like a tree planted by the rivers of water, that bringeth forth his fruit in his season."

—Psalms 1:3

"For the earth bringeth forth fruit of herself; *first the blade, then the ear,* after that *the full corn in the ear.*"

—Mark 4:28

"The Lord hath sought him a man after his own heart."

—1 Samuel 13:14

## FIRST THE BLADE

## THEN THE EAR

## THE FULL CORN IN THE EAR

# Table of Contents

# Saul's Early World

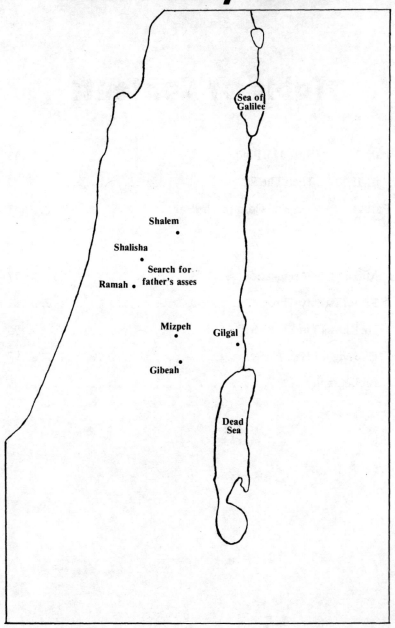

Sea of
Galilee

Shalem

Shalisha

Search for
father's asses

Ramah

Mizpeh

Gilgal

Gibeah

Dead
Sea

## Part I
# First The Blade

## 1 Samuel 8:1 - 20:42

I. The Anointing Of David By Samuel At Bethlehem

II. David's World
  A. Brief summation of the history of Israel up to this time
  B. Selection of Saul
  C. Early characteristics of Saul
  D. Incidents reflecting a change of Saul's attitude
    1. Erroneous offering of a sacrifice at Gilgal
    2. Incident of depriving Israelites of food and severity of Jonathan's proposed punishment
    3. Disobedience in treatment of Amalekites

III. David At Saul's Court
  A. Reasons for selection
  B. Advantages

IV. Encounter With Goliath
  A. Description of Goliath
  B. Reasons for David's presence
  C. Ridicule by Eliab
  D. The battle

V. David's Permanent Residence At Saul's Court
  A. Friendship with Jonathan
  B. Women's praise of David which precipitated Saul's jealousy and outbursts of temper
  C. Saul's efforts to have David killed
    1. Offer of Mereb as wife
    2. Terms for hand of Michal
    3. Commands given to Jonathan and servants
    4. Javelin thrown at court
    5. Plot at the house of David and Michal
    6. Temporary escape to Samuel at Ramah
  D. Meeting of David and Jonathan with the resulting covenant

13

# David's Early World

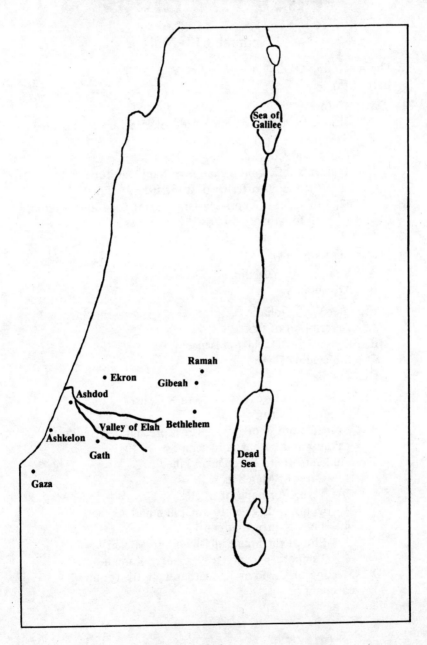

Sea of Galilee

Ramah

Ekron

Gibeah

Ashdod

Bethlehem

Valley of Elah

Ashkelon

Gath

Dead Sea

Gaza

## Part I

# First The Blade

It must have been a very exciting day in the little village of Bethlehem when Samuel arrived from the neighboring town of Ramah (about ten miles away). This man who was the last of the judges and the transitional figure between the judges and the kings of Israel (1 Samuel 7:15), in addition to being both a priest and a prophet (2 Chronicles 35:18), had caused the elders of the town to tremble over the reason for their leader's mission. After assuring them that he had come to offer a sacrifice, Samuel especially requested the presence of one particular family - Jesse and his sons. Evidently the task of God's spokesman was shrouded in mystery, but it was apparent that he was looking for a special person. When Jesse's eldest son, Eliab, passed in front of Samuel, the young man's countenance must have been impressive for Samuel thought that this must surely be the Lord's anointed. But he was rejected.

(1) *Why* (1 Samuel 16:7)?

As the other sons passed before the priest, God rejected them one by one. Samuel no doubt became worried. Had not God sent him to this little village of Bethlehem for the express purpose of anointing one of the sons of Jesse to be the next king of Israel? None of these young men seemed acceptable to Jehovah. What was he to do now? He must have asked Jesse in exasperation, "Are here all thy children?" No, there was one more. The youngest had not even been asked to attend this village event. After all, someone had to remain with the sheep. It was only natural to leave the youngest one to perform this routine task. Nevertheless, upon Samuel's insistence, David was fetched.

(2) *What were the three phrases used to describe David at this time of his life* (1 Samuel 16:12)?

After the anointing of Jesse's youngest in the midst of his brethren, Samuel left; but the spirit of the Lord came upon David from that day forward.

(3) *Do you suppose that David's father and brothers fully understood the significance of the anointing? Why?*

## David's World

Very simply God ended the details of this monumental occasion. Samuel left Bethlehem and went to Ramah. David returned to his customary tasks of caring for the sheep. King Saul, unaware of the events which had just transpired, continued to rule from his rather crude fortress palace at Gibeah, only seven miles from Bethlehem.

Thus concludes our introduction to David, the young shepherd son of Jesse. No child has ever been born in a vacuum. The circumstances prevalent in the surrounding world necessarily had their effect upon this young life. The student needs to understand David's *world* before he can begin to unravel the threads of David's *personal life.*

David was born toward the end of the eleventh century B.C. An approximate dating of the beginning of the patriarchal age would safely lie between 2,000 to 1,508 B.C. Much had transpired between the calling of Abraham and God's promise to make a great nation of his descendants until this moment in Israel's history. Abraham, Isaac, and Jacob had lived rather prosperous nomadic lives before Jacob's sons temporarily journeyed to Egypt in search of food and eventually lived there for approximately four hundred years. Moses then guided his people through forty years of wilderness wanderings, followed by Joshua, who led the Israelites into the promised land to conquer the hostile people living there. Here God's people gradually occupied the underpopulated heights of Canaan, but most of the walled fortress towns of the Canaanites on the Coast defied capture. It was a loosely joined confederation of tribes, each removed from the other by geographical boundaries. Tribalism, which had been the way of life during the forty years of desert wanderings, naturally suited this nomadic nation. Upon the death of Joshua, different judges were selected at various times by Jehovah to settle judicial matters and deliver the people from oppressors with the assistance of tribal militia during emergencies. Although this was God's chosen plan of government, the nation deteriorated into a general state of lawlessness during which time "every man did that which was right in his own eyes" (Judges 21:25). Corruption was personified in the two sons of Samuel:

"And his sons walked not in his ways, but turned aside after lucre, and took bribes, and perverted judgment" (1 Samuel 8:3). Following this experience the people demanded: "Now make us a king to judge us like all the nations" (1 Samuel 8:5). Thus, corruption, ever increasing enemies, and lack of faith in God prompted the Israelites to ask for a form of government not ordained by Jehovah.

Towering above his fellowman, Saul seemed to be a natural choice (1 Samuel 9:2). Anointed secretly by Samuel while looking for Kish's lost asses, Saul met his first challenge when the Ammonites threatened the people of Jabesh-gilead.

(4) *What was the ultimatum given to them?* (See 1 Samuel 11:1-4)

Saul's leadership seemed to be clearly established with this victory. Two years later the observant student can detect a change in Saul's attitude at Gilgal when his forces faced the Philistines gathered in Michmash.

(5) *What was the King's sin?* (See Samuel 13:8-13.)

(6) *At this time God indicated that he would begin searching for a new leader, a man after ___ own heart.* (Note 1 Samuel 13:14 and also Acts 13:22.)

(7) *What does this phrase mean?*

(8) *What unreasonable demand did Saul make of his men?* (See 1 Samuel 14:24.)

(9) *How would you evaluate the king's reasoning regarding the proposed punishment of Jonathan, his own son?* (Read 1 Samuel 14:43-54.)

(10) *Contrast this attitude with Saul's earlier mercy when some wanted to put dissenters to death.* (See 1 Samuel 12:12-13.)

Saul's behavior when sent on a mission to kill all the Amalekites was certainly not characteristics of a man of God.

(11) *At this time what was Saul's sin which caused God to repent that Saul had been made king over Israel?* (See 1 Samuel 15:1-23.)

(12) *Summarize the three previously discussed transgressions that indicate a change in Saul's attitude.*

Thus, in David's immediate world we can see the decline of a king which God never wanted in the first place. From the time of the judges until we first meet David, the Israelites had effectively met the advances of the Moabites, Ammonites, and other trans-Jordanian people; but the Philistines still posed a powerful threat. Internationally there was a power vacuum. During this time neither Egypt nor the Hittites were major powers. The Assyrian threat was still in the future. The possibilities of Israel's becoming a strong power were great, *if* the Philistines could be controlled. Since Saul seemed inept for various reasons, including the three stated above, a new leader was needed. David was God's selection.

> He chose David also his servant, and took him from the sheepfolds: from following the ewes great with young he brought him to feed Jacob his people, and Israel his inheritance. So he fed them according to the integrity of his heart; and guided them by the skillfulness of his hands.
>
> Psalms 78:70-72

### Why David?

The man who later became the most beloved king of Israel began as a common shepherd boy. Yet Samuel's anointing singled out the specific person from whom Christ would later come. (Note Psalms 89:20, Luke 1:32, and Acts 2:30).

(12) *Why does God choose the weak things of the world to confound the things that are mighty?* (See 1 Corinthians 1:27-31).

(13) *Further illustrate this principle in the examples of the cleansing of Naaman and also baptism.*

(14) *What was there in David's background at this present time that formed the matrix for the shaping of a man after God's own heart? (Consider the solitude of the shepherd's life, which stimulated David's imagination and undoubtedly had its effect upon his poetical sensitivity and his musical ability. This close communion with nature is reflected in Psalms 19. Also consider the responsibility placed upon his shoulders, his skill in the use of simple weapons, his bravery in the killing of the lion and the bear, his loyalty to his sheep, and even his braving the elements of nature.)*

### At Saul's Court

After the anointing by Samuel, David resumed the duties of a shepherd. Seven miles away at his fortress type dwelling at Gibeah, King Saul continued ruling Israel and fighting the Philistines. (Note the changes in his personality.) When Samuel sought Saul for the public anointing, the young man was so timid that he hid himself among the baggage. Anger motivated his assertion of power later as he summoned help for the people of Jabesh-gilead. A taste of authority can become intoxicating. This feeling of omnipotence prompted Saul's refusal to allow his people to eat while in battle and even precipitated the threat of his own son's life for eating honey! A feeling of his own importance caused him to disobey God in offering sacrifices and also in sparing the life of King Agag. Highs are usually followed by lows. Evidently Saul suffered periods of extreme depression. "But the Spirit of the Lord departed from Saul, and an evil spirit from the Lord troubled him" (1 Samuel 16:14). Note the events in the King's rebellion that were indicative of this reversal.

(15) *What suggestion was made by Saul's servants?* (See 1 Samuel 16:16.)

(16) *David's reputation as a musician influenced his selection as Saul's musician. What were some of David's traits of character which could have been instrumental?* (Read 1 Samuel 16:18).

(17) *What was Saul's reaction to David? What was David's official position?* (See 1 Samuel 16:21.) *Do you suppose that David experienced any fear at this time? Consider the possibility that Saul could have learned of the anointing. David very easily could have been walking into a trap set for him.*

(18) *How did David's position at the court of Saul help to prepare him for the duties of a king later?*

(19) *Although David was Saul's armor-bearer and court musician, did he remain at Saul's palace all the time?* (Note 1 Samuel 17:15.) *Evidently God felt that His chosen one needed more lessons to be learned as a shepherd.*

### Encounter with Goliath

As the next stage of the narrative unfolds, we find Saul and his army arrayed for battle against the Philistines at the valley of Elah in the foothills of the Judean mountains.

The Philistines were part of a group known as the Sea People. They had already overwhelmed the Hittite Empire about 1200 B.C. Next they invaded Egypt during the reigns of Merneptah (1224-1216 B.C.) and Ramses III (1174-1144 B.C.). This latter ruler spent most of his time trying to keep the Sea Peoples from overwhelming Egypt. One of these tribes was called Tjekker and another was known as Peleset. Driven out of Egypt, they were allowed to settle in Palestine as guardians of Egyptian interests and became known as the Philistines, from which the name Palestine was derived. In the meantime Egypt's world power was declining. Although she still claimed Palestine, she had no power to enforce laws. The reigns of Ramses IV to XI (1144-1065) were short. It was during this period of weak Egyptian rule that the judges ruled Israel. Since there was no other mighty power to assume the leadership, there was a power vacuum in western Asia. The Hittite Empire in Asia Minor had fallen before the Sea Peoples around 1200 B.C. Assyria's greatness was still in the future. Thus, Western Asia was made up of warring smaller states but there was no dominant power. In Palestine the Philistines' main occupancy was in the southern coastal regions in the form of a confederation of five cities: Gaza, Ashkelon, Ashdod, Ekron, and Gath. Their territory stretched from Gaza to the outskirts of modern Tel Aviv and inland to Bethshan. Having adopted many Canaanite ways and gods, these Philistines dominated the western fringe of the land. Much lay at stake in this battle.

Three of David's older brothers (Eliab, Abinadab, and Shammah) were in the army of Israel.

(20) *Why did David go to the battlefront?* (See 1 Samuel 17:17-18.) *When David heard the excitement, he left the food with the keeper of the baggage and ran to the front ranks.*

(21) *What was the cause of all the commotion?* (Read 1 Samuel 17:23-27.)

(22) *What sort of challenge had Goliath previously offered?*(Note 1 Samuel 17:8-10.)

(23) *For how many days was the offer made?* (See 1 Samuel 17:16.)

(24) *After examining 1 Samuel 17:4-7, describe Goliath:*
Height: _____ cubits and a span
(Clark's Commentary - 9 feet and 9 inches tall)
*Are there records of earlier giants?* (See Genesis 6:4; Numbers 13:34; Deuteronomy 2:11; Deuteronomy 3:11,13; Joshua 12:4; Joshua 13:12.)

(25) *Why do you suppose that Goliath did not carry his own shield?*

Although Saul promised to make the victor of Goliath rich, give him the King's own daughter and make his house free, David's primary motivation seemed to be found in his desire to rid the armies of the living God of this threat. Eliab, David's oldest brother, was quite skeptical of David's ability as the younger brother was belittled in the presence of others.

(26) *How did David prove his ability to Saul?* (See verses 34-37.)

(27) *How did Saul equip David for battle?* (Read verses 38 and 39.)

(28) *Why did David reject Saul's offer?* (Note verse 39 and also Zechariah 4:6.) *What would be the disadvantages of using unfamiliar armor?*

(29) *Why do you suppose David took five stones instead of only one? Does this indicate a lack of faith? Why were smooth stones chosen?*

(30) *According to verses 40-54, describe the battle which took place.*

(31) *What was there in David's previous training that proved to be beneficial at this time?*

(32) *Saul had previously loved David greatly and had even sent for permission to have David live with him* (1 Samuel 16:21,22). *Why did he not even know who David was at this time* (1 Samuel 17:55-58)?

## Dark Clouds Gather

After the battle with Goliath, Saul would not allow David to return home. It was during this period of time that David and Jonathan developed a very close friendship.

(33) *Describe the outward manifestations of this covenant* (1 Samuel 18:1-4).

When Saul set David over the men of war, the youth behaved himself wisely and was accepted by both the servants and the people. It has always been a fairly simple matter to weep with those who are down and out, but rejoicing with the successful is a different matter. As the women openly lauded Israel's new hero, jealousy reared its ugly head and stirred the coals of anger within Saul's mind. "And Saul eyed David from that day and forward" (1 Samuel 18:9). This incident seems to have been a turning point in the narrative, for David had nothing but trouble from that time on.

(34) *Do you feel that Samuel's prophecy in 1 Samuel 15:23,26,28 was bearing on Saul's mind at this time? Since Saul had asked for forgiveness in 1 Samuel 15:25, why do you suppose that his sin has not been pardoned?*

Saul's disruptive behavior (a symptom of paranoia) is evidenced in his violent outbursts of temper, such as throwing a javelin while David played. The King got the court musician out of his sight by making him captain over a thousand men. Still David behaved himself wisely.

(35) *What was the ulterior motive behind Saul's offer of his daughter Merab to David as a wife* (1 Samuel 18:17)? *What was David's answer* (1 Samuel 18:18)?

Alas, Merab's sister, Michal, fell in love with the mighty warrior. Saul seized upon this opportunity to trap David.

**(36)** *What was the offer and the ulterior motive (1 Samuel 18:20-25)? What were the results? Why did David accept the offer of Michal and not Merab?*

When Saul saw that the Lord was with David and that Michal loved him, the King became even more afraid of the young man. Since several schemes had failed, Saul next turned to the more direct approach and openly asked Jonathan and all the servants to kill David.

**(37)** *With what line of reasoning did Jonathan answer (1 Samuel 19:4-7)?*

Although Jonathan's arguments brought the situation back to what appeared to be normal, the evil spirit came upon Saul and he responded by again trying to smite David to the wall with the javelin. David fled to his own home and escaped the next morning from Saul's messengers. (Psalms 59 is said to reflect David's feelings at this time.)

**(38)** *How did Michal aid in David's escape by preparing a decoy under the bed clothes according to 1 Samuel 19:11-17? Can her deceit be justified?*

**(39)** *Describe the strange events which transpired when David fled to Samuel at Naioth in Ramah as they are recorded in verses 18-24 of 1 Samuel 19. (Saul's strange behavior gave David ample time to escape.)*

David and Jonathan had another secret meeting during which it was decided that Jonathan would again plead his friend's case before Saul because David realized that "there is but a step between me and death" (1 Samuel 20:3). He chose the time for a yearly family feast in Bethlehem as an excuse for not being at the King's table. Jonathan was to report his father's reaction by signaling with arrows close to the place where David would be hiding. If Saul was amiable, then Jonathan would shoot an arrow and say to the lad, "Behold, the arrows are on this side of thee." The opposite response would be indicated in the instructions: "Behold, the arrows are beyond thee." At the feast Saul was angry over David's absence - *very angry.* When Jonathan gave the prearranged signal, the two steadfast friends embraced with the promise that the Lord would be between them and their seed. It must have been a very touching scene. Just as the arrows were beyond the lad, so was the kingdom beyond David; but both he and Jonathan knew that it would one day belong to this humble son of Jesse. They must have sensed the blood and struggle involved. At this point try to step into David's shoes. He had been promised the kingdom. Although he had behaved bravely and wisely, the prospects must have looked very dim. If you had been David, would you have had enough faith to believe the promise which we have in Romans 8:28 that all things would eventually work together for good for those who love God? If you had been in Jonathan's place, could you have maintained the right attitude toward your dearest friend when you knew that what should have been your kingdom by inheritance would one day belong to David?

## Summary of the Blade Years

Our study began with the anointing of a young boy who would one day replace Saul as King of Israel. The rugged life of a shepherd, in addition to the inherent peace and quiet of the occupation ("In quietness and in confidence shall be your strength"—Isaiah 30:15), had already begun its shaping of this new national leader. Also, David would need physical stamina during the next period of his existence as he literally ran for his life. He would also need the spiritual strength which had slowly been building within him as he communed with Jehovah on those lonely Judean hills day in and day out as he cared for his sheep. The time spent at King Saul's court must have been mixed with joy and sorrow. Here he learned to love Jonathan. Here he witnessed the violent displays of the King's temper; but here he also became knowledgeable concerning the govenment of Israel, which must have been of great value in later years.

Thus far David had behaved wisely and truly had done nothing to his discredit. The next segment of his life was to be a period of severe testing (Psalms 11:5). David's patience, faith, and humility had to be proven before he was given greater opportunities. Let's follow the inspired pages as we learn the importance of these years.

# David's Middle Years

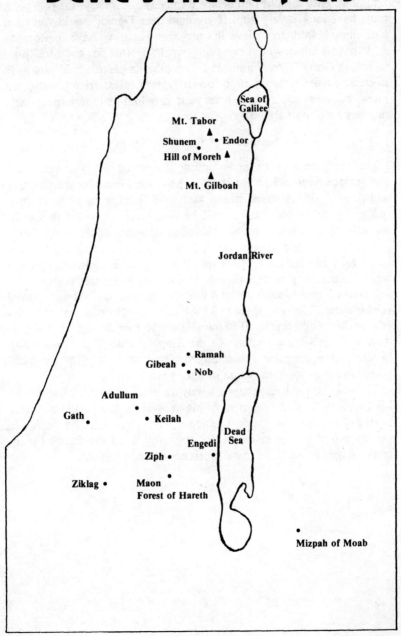

# Part II

# Then The Ear —
# The Crucible of Testing

### (1 Samuel 21:1 - 2 Samuel 1:27)
**Mountain Peaks and Valleys in David's Flight from Saul**

| | | |
|---|---|---|
| I. | *Nob* (1 Samuel 21:1-9) | Food and Goliath's sword given to David by Ahimelech the priest |
| II. | *Gath* (1 Samuel 21:10-15) | Madness feigned by David to escape Achish |
| III. | *Cave of Adullum* (1 Samuel 22:1-4 ) | Four hundred followers attracted by David |
| IV. | *Forest of Hareth* (1 Samuel 22:5) | David's next refuge |
| V. | *Gibeah* (1 Samuel 22:6-23) | The slaying of Ahimelech and all his house by Doeg |
| VI. | *Keilah* (1 Samuel 23:1-14) | Town spared defeat at the hands of the Philistines by David and his men |
| VII. | *Wilderness of Ziph* (1 Samuel 23:15-18) | Final meeting of David and Jonathan |
| VIII. | *Gibeah* (1 Samuel 23:19-23) | Saul told of David's location by the inhabitants of Ziph |
| IX. | *Wilderness of Moan* (1 Samuel 23:24-28) | David spared attack by Saul when the King was informed of an immediate attack by the Philistines |
| X. | *Strongholds at Engedi* (1 Samuel 23:29-24:22) | Saul spared by David in a cave at Engedi |
| XI. | *The Wilderness of Paran* (1 Samuel 25:1-43) | David's encounter with Nabal and subsequent marriage to Abigail |
| XII. | *The Wilderness of Ziph* (1 Samuel 26:1-25) | David's sparing of the life of the sleeping king |
| XIII. | *Gath* (1 Samuel 27:1-4) | Philistine refuge sought by David and his followers |
| XIV. | *Ziklag* (1 Samuel 27:5 - 28:2) | Village given to David for occupany by Achish, King of Gath, and base for raids |

| | | |
|---|---|---|
| | | upon the enemies of Israel |
| XV. | *Shunem, Gilboa, and Endor* (1 Samuel 28:3-29:11) | Saul's encounter with the woman at Endor as the Philistines and the Israelites gathered for battle |
| XVI. | *Ziklag* (1 Samuel 30:1-31) | Recovery of all the inhabitants who were taken captive by the Amalekites |
| XVII. | *Gilboa* (1 Samuel 31:1-13) | Defeat of Israel and death of Saul |
| XVIII. | *Ziklag* (2 Samuel 1:1-27) | Messenger bearing news of Saul's death ordered to be killed by David |

## Part II

# Then The Ear—
# The Crucible of Testing

### The Storm Bursts Forth

Until this time we have watched spellbound while the threads of David's life have been woven to form the character of a young man truly after God's own heart as these traits became apparent:

(1) *A close communion with God on those lonely Judean hillsides* — The lad watched the clouds, the green grass and the trickling streams as he meditated upon the Word of God and talked with his heavenly Father.

(2) *Faithfulness and obedience to his responsibilities* — Note the manner in which he accepted the care of the sheep when Samuel came to Bethlehem at the time of the anointing and the lad's return to his duties as a shepherd when this last judge left. Also, David displayed the same characteristic as he killed wild animals in protecting his sheep (1 Samuel 17:34-37). Even when he left home to carry food to his fighting brothers, he was faithful to his responsibilities in leaving the care of his sheep with a keeper (1 Samuel 17:20).

(3) *Development of needed skills* — The early period of David's life was not merely the passing of time. Days and months and even years of practice made David quite skillful with a sling as he protected his precious sheep from wild animals. When the youth stepped before Goliath, God was certainly with the lad as the stone was hurled through the air to the most vulnerable spot on the giant; but the accuracy was not entirely miraculous. David, the expert marksman, depended upon God's care; but he had also faithfully prepared himself. It was during the early days as a shepherd that David became quite adept at playing the harp to pass away the time on the lonely Judean hillsides. He had done his part and was ready when the King called for a skilled musician to ease mental strains. It was also during these early years that David developed the ability to bear the iniquities of his brothers with grace (1 Samuel 17:28-29).

(4) *Faith and reliance upon God* — David had prepared himself with the needed skills to kill Goliath, but he was also aware of his human frailities and depended upon God for the victory.

(5) *Humbleness and obedience* — David displayed obedience as he returned to his duties as a shepherd after he had been anointed as the next king of Israel. Even after his selection as the King's musician, the youth fulfilled family obligations as he once again assumed his original responsibilities. David's humbleness is evidenced in his refusal of the offer of Saul's daughter Merab as a wife because he felt unworthy (1 Samuel 18:18, 23).

(6) *Good conduct* — Over and over the same thread runs throughout the record of David's early years. No matter what test of character to which David was subjected, the same result is noted time and again - he behaved himself wisely.

(7) *Cultivation of a friendship with a faithful child of God* — Jonathan's friendship (a genuine respect of both parties) had already proved beneficial in saving David's life and continued to be of help (both physically and emotionally) for years to come.

David's early character is succinctly summarized in the eighteenth verse of the sixteenth chapter of 1 Samuel: "Then answered one of the servants, and said, "Behold, I have seen a son of Jesse the Bethlehemite, that is cunning in playing, and a mighty valiant man, and a man of war, and prudent in matters, and a comely person, and the Lord is with him.''


During those early years David's strengths far outnumbered any human weaknesses which he inevitably must have had, for no mention is made of the latter. The next phase of the shepherd's life was truly the crucible of testing when David encountered some of the most difficult hurdles of his existence as he literally ran for his life for approximately ten years in and out of the valleys and hillsides of Israel. The arrow of kingship had been shot before the lad. Although promised and in the future, the time for its possession lay ahead. For literally years Saul sought David every day (1 Samuel 23:14) as one hunts a partridge in the mountain (1 Samuel 26:20). "Flee as a bird to your mountain" is not only a line from a beautiful hymn; the words also describe David's manner of life (Psalms 11:1). In trying to follow David during this period of time, the most logical manner seems to be to pause for a few moments at each geographical stop and view the events which transpired there.

## Nob (1 Samuel 21:1-9)

As it is usually characteristic of a true child of God, David's first stop in his flight from Saul was to a man of God - the priest Ahimelech at Nob, a village near Gibeah and about twelve miles from Jerusalem. It was here that the tabernacle had been pitched and was the dwelling place of eighty-six priests. Perhaps David felt that he could consider his next moves in peace and quiet at this place.

(1) *Upon their meeting, why did the priest Ahimelech ask David whether or not he was alone when it was quite evident that some young men accompanied David (1 Samuel 21:1)?*

(2) *Why did David tell Ahimelech an obvious lie about his mission (1 Samuel 21:2)?*

Upon asking for food, David and his men were given showbread from the tabernacle. (Read Matthew 12:1-8 to determine Christ's evaluation of this event.)

David also requested a weapon. (Note another lie mentioned in verse 8.) Ironically, the only weapon there was the sword of Goliath, wrapped in a cloth behind the ephod. David took the weapon and fled to Gath.

(3) *Do you suppose the presence of Doeg (Saul's chief herdman mentioned in verse seven) could have had any influence upon David's fear of Achish? (Read ahead in 1 Samuel 22:9-22.)*

## Gath (1 Samuel 21:10-15)

With showbread for food and the sword of Goliath as his weapon, David next fled to Gath, a Philistine village near the coast and the home of Goliath. Evidently David was well known throughout the land for his acts of bravery because the people mentioned David's feats to Achish, the kings of Gath.

(4) *What possible rationale could be given for David's fleeing to the very town of the giant whom he had killed? (Remember that David was carrying Goliath's sword with him as a weapon.)*

Fear prompted David to pretend madness before the people of Gath in order to escape.

(5) *What two physical characteristics do the Scriptures mention (1 Samuel 21:13)?*

(6) *Was this feigned madness a false pretense? Can you give any justification for David's deceit and hypocrisy?*

29

(7) *Some have supposed that Psalm 56 was based upon this incident and also Psalm 34. Read them and give your opinion.* Note the tender expression in verse 8 of Psalm 56: "Put thou my tears into thy bottle." If verses 12-14 of Psalm 34 seem familiar to you, see 1 Peter 3:10. Also, note David's dependence upon God in verse 18: "The Lord is nigh unto them that are of a broken heart and saveth such as be of a contrite spirit."

## Cave of Adullam (1 Samuel 22:1-4)

The fugitive escaped from Gath to a a cave situated near the fortress like hill called Adullam in the unclaimed wilderness near the border between Judah and the territory of the Philistines where he attracted a band of about four hundred followers, some of whom were his relatives. The Scriptures give three characteristics of this following (1 Samuel 22:2): those who were in distress, in debt, and discontented. (It doesn't sound like a very favorable group of supporters upon which to depend, does it?)

(8) *Which types of people are usually the most receptive to the Gospel today?*

(9) *Note David's plea for the safety in the "shadow of thy wings" at this time* (Psalms 57:1).

(10) *To what depth of despair had he dropped* (Psalms 142:4)?

David's concern for his father and mother prompted his request to the king of Moab for their safety during the exile period. (The reader will recall that David had Moabite blood in him through Ruth.)

(11) *Why were David's parents in danger?*

(David's love and care are examples of his strengths during this period of his life.) The prophet Gad told David to depart from the hold to the land of Judah.

## Forest of Hareth in the Land of Judah (1 Samuel 22:5)

After leaving the hold at the cave of Adullum, David was instructed to depart to the forest of Hareth.

## Gibeah (1 Samuel 22:6-23)

The scene of action leaves David in the forest of Hareth and switches to Saul at his home in Gibeah. Poor Saul, sitting under a tree with a spear in his hand, was just about as depressed as Elijah under a juniper tree! The ruler trusted no one, telling his men that they had conspired against him in failing to inform him of the league between David and Jonathan. Note Saul's mental deterioration in the sentence: "There is none of you that is sorry for me" (1 Samuel 22:8). Capitalizing upon Saul's insecurity and paranoid mental condition, Doeg the Edomite pounced upon the opportunity by telling all that he had seen and overheard at Nob when David and his men received bread and Goliath's sword from the priest Ahimelech. (Knowing human nature, are you really surprised at Doeg's move?) When Ahimelech and the others were called before Saul, the priest gave a very logical explanation.

(12) *What was Ahimelech's line of reasoning in explaining his action (1 Samuel 22:14-15)?*

(13) *When Saul commanded his servants to kill Ahimelech and all his house, how did the former react (1 Samuel 22:17)?*

(14) *Describe Doeg's ruthless action, including the slaying of every living person and animal at Nob (1 Samuel 22:18-19).*

Abiathar, one of the sons of Ahimelech, escaped to the safety of David's refuge and told him all that had happened.

(15) *What does David's attitude in verse 22 tell the reader about a strength in his character?*

(16) *Psalms 52 is said to have been prompted by the events which have just transpired. After reading it, do you think David's feelings were justified?*

### Keilah (1 Samuel 23:1-13)

Shortly after hearing the heartbreaking news of the recent slaughter from Abiathar the priest, another problem reared its ugly head. It was reported to David that the Philistines were robbing the threshing floors of Keilah, a fortified town in the tribe of Judah on the road to Hebron. In those days the threshing floors were located in open fields and were thus vulnerable to attacks.

(17) *Saul was King. Why do you suppose that he did not come to the aid of his people in Keilah at this time?*

When David inquired of the Lord, He instructed His servant to smite the Philistines and save the town. David's men were fearful of the Philistines, so the leader of the group once again asked God's advice and received an affirmative answer. Complete victory was the result.

When Saul learned of the situation, he must have gleefully thought about victory over David and his men since they were as caged animals within the city walls. While Saul readied his soldiers for attack, David had the foresight to take advantage of Abiathar's ephod to ask God whether or not the men of Keilah would deliver David and his men into the land of Saul.

(18) *Use reference books to learn what an ephod was and how it was used.*

God's answer was quite clear. Yes, the men of Keilah would deliver David and his men into Saul's hands.

(19) *What does this tell you about human nature?*

## Wilderness of Ziph (1 Samuel 23:14-18)

Resorting to the only sensible course of action, David and his followers fled to mountainous strongholds in the wilderness of Ziph. Verse fourteen contains six words portending unrelenting fear and stress: "And Saul sought him every day," but the next part of the verse very comfortingly supplies the answer to any problem: "But God delivered him not into his hand." Try to place yourself in David's shoes and imagine the inevitable feeling of awakening each morning with the realization that Saul and his men could be lying in wait behind every hill or any other hiding place in the land - ready to pounce upon God's anointed at any moment. And we think we live in a stressful era! It was at this place, without fanfare and show, that the King's son entered upon the scene and "strengthened his hand in God" (verse 16).

(20) *What were the inherent dangers in Jonathan's appearance in the midst of the stronghold of his father's enemies?*

It almost brings tears to one's eyes when he reads Jonathan's reassuring word to David: "Fear not: for the hand of Saul my father shall not find thee; and thou shalt be king over Israel, and I shall be next unto thee . . . "

(21) *Try to step into Jonathan's shoes. The throne would legally and rightfully have been his, yet his submission to God's will prompted these comforting words to David. Could you have been so magnanimous that you would have sincerely uttered such a statement to David?*

Just as quietly as he had slipped into David's stronghold, Jonathan crept back to his home. According to the Scriptures, the two never met again on this earth.

## Gibeah (1 Samuel 23:19-23)

David had been hiding in the wilderness of Ziph. The inhabitants of Ziph informed Saul of David's location in the strongholds in the wood and in the hills of the wilderness of Ziph on the south of Jeshimon. The offering of these inhabitants to assist Saul in his search must have boosted his ego, "for ye have compassion on me" (verse 21).

(22) *Compare Saul's need for flattery with his pouting attitude in 1 Samuel 22:8.*

Saul sent the men on a mission to search for David. After they had located the fugitive, Saul planned the capture.

(23) *Psalms 54 is said to have been written at this time. Read it to gain deeper insight into David's feelings.*

## Wilderness of Maon (1 Samuel 23:24-28)

David certainly had enough sense to flee from his pursuers when he left Ziph and went to the wilderness of Maon in the plain on the south of Jeshimon. Keilah had refused him safety. The Ziphites had betrayed him. Like a partridge, he played hide-and-seek with Saul among the mountains of this wilderness area. At one point David and his men had encamped on one side of the mountain while Saul and his forces were on the other side, making ready to encompass the enemy. At the crucial moment when Saul planned to attack, the ruler received word that the Philistines had invaded the land. Such a national state of emergency was more important than pursuing a fugitive, so Saul and his men abandoned their favored position and left to defend the land.

(24) *Do you feel that David and his men would have escaped from their precarious location had it not been for the invasion of the Philistines at this precise moment? State your reasons.*

## Strongholds at Engedi (1 Samuel 23:29 - 24:22)

Engedi, located about midway on the western shore of the Dead Sea, must have been a very rugged and deserted refuge. It was not only called a wilderness, but reference was also made to the rocks of the wild goats. (Sheep-cotes were spacious caves in the rocks where shepherds and their flocks lodged.) After Saul had alleviated the threat of the Philistines, he and three thousand of his chosen soldiers resumed the task of searching for the partridge in the mountains of the wilderness of Engedi (1 Samuel 26:20).

33

(25) *Pause to let the entire class join in the singing of "Flee As A Bird To Your Mountain"\* (Psalms 11:1).*

While David and his men were hidden along the sides of a cave at Engedi, Saul entered. David's men urged their leader to take advantage of the King's vulnerable position. God's appointed did cut off a part of Saul's robe, but remorse overwhelmed David.

(26) *What was the reason for David's regret (1 Samuel 24:6)? Do you think David's attitude was a wise one? What would your reaction have been?*

David restrained his men, and Saul went on his way unaware of the danger from which he had narrowly escaped.

*(27) Some Bible scholars maintain that the writing of Psalms 57 and 142 is supposedly based upon this instance. Others feel that these Psalms refer to the happenings at the cave of Adullum (1 Samuel 22:1-4). What is your opinion? Could the thoughts be applicable to both?*

(28) *After Saul had left the cave, David called after his king. Briefly express his message in your own words* (1 Samuel 24:8-15).

(29) *What strength of character does David display in this discourse?*

Saul wept upon hearing David's words, admitting that David was more righteous than himself because the former shepherd had rewarded the King good for evil by refusing to kill him when there was ample opportunity.

(30) *Do you think Saul was sincere?*

(31) *What inevitable event did Saul admit?* (See verse 20.) *What sort of emotion do you feel that this statement must have evoked in Saul?*

(32) *Saul made a request of David. What was it?* (See verse 21.)

(33) *Keep this promise in mind for future reasons which lay behind some of David's actions.*

The Scripture very simply closes this most dramatic encounter with the statement: "And Saul went home; but David and his men got them up unto the hold."

*Found in Great Songs of the Church

## The Wilderness of Paran - Nabal and Abigail (1 Samuel 25:1-43)

The exciting narration of this period of David's life was interrupted by the simple statement that Samuel died and was buried in his house at Ramah (verse 1).

David and his men retreated to the wilderness of Paran (between the mountains of Judah and Mt. Sinai near Maon in the plain situated on the south of Jeshimon). It is in this setting that one of the most exciting (but often unnoticed) narrations in the Scriptures unfolds. Living in this area was Nabal from the same tribe as David and a descendant of Caleb. Evidently he was a man of considerable wealth.

*(34) Support this conclusion with facts from 1 Samuel 25:2.*

*(35) Contrast the qualities of Nabal and his wife Abigail (verse 3). What is the meaning of the word churlish?*

*(36) Discuss the unusual, but beautiful, combination of characteristics which Abigail possessed.*

David sent his messengers to Nabal with a courteous request for provisions for his men. It was the season for shearing the sheep. Since it was the custom to combine feasting with shearing (2 Samuel 13:23 and Genesis 38:13), there was undoubtedly an ample supply of food prepared. It was a time of hospitality.

*(37) By what right did David feel that he could request food of Nabal (verse 6-8)?*

*(38) Do you think David was justified in this request?*

*(39) Have you ever wondered how David managed daily to feed his tremendously large following of men during the years of darting from one hiding place to another?*

Nabal's reply should have been expected from a man of his disposition (verse 3). "Who is David? And who is the son of Jesse? There be many servants nowadays that break away every man from his master. Shall I then take *my* bread, and *my* water, and *my* flesh that I have killed for *my* shearers, and give it unto men, whom I know not whence they be?" (verse 11). Needless to say, David was angered by the reply. Upon hearing the news, he left two hundred men to guard the possessions, girded on his sword, and departed with four hundred others to encounter this rude, arrogant desert leader.

*(40) Contrast David's petulance and destructive plans with his reverence for the life of Saul in chapter 24.*

One of Nabal's men learned of the approaching entourage and hastened to Abigail, warning her of the imminent danger and also of the good which David had done for Nabal's men.

(41) *List the ways in which David and his men had aided Nabal's men* (verses 14-17).

(42) *What is the meaning of the term: "They were a 'wall' unto us both by night and day, all the while we were with them keeping the sheep"* (verse 16)?

Abigail was a woman of action! Sensing the danger, she hastened to make amends to David and his men for the insulting manner of her husband.

(43) *How much food did she prepare for David's group* (verses 18, 19)?

(44) *Why did she take so much? Why did she instruct the servants to go ahead of her* (verse 19)?

Just as Abigail rounded the hill, whom should she meet face to face but David and his men! Jumping off her donkey, she bowed her face to the ground.

(45) *Outline Abigail's plea* (verses 24-31).

(46) *Note the beautiful figurative language used in verse 29: "But the soul of my lord shall be bound in the bundle of life with the Lord thy God."*

(47) *What effect did Abigail's approach have upon David's attitude* (verses 32-35)?

(48) *What is the implied lesson for us today in dealing with our enemies?*

When Abigail returned home, she found that Nabal had really thrown a drunken brawl. In fact, he was so drunk that she told him nothing until the next morning. When she talked with her husband, "his heart died within him and he became as a stone." After ten days the Lord smote Nabal and he died.

(49) *What do you think is the meaning of the phrase: "his heart died within him and he became as a stone"?*

Learning of Nabal's death, David sent for Abigail to become his wife. During this wilderness wandering period, David also married Ahinoam of Jezreel (verse 43). Some think that David took Ahinoam before Abigail because the former is always mentioned first in the list of wives and was the mother of the eldest son, Ammon.

(50) *Was there any justification for David's having these two wives* (verse 43)?

(51) *What had happened to Michal, David's first wife* (verse 44)? *Was she still his wife?*

## The Wilderness of Ziph (1 Samuel 26:1-25)

Always on the run, David next hid himself in the wilderness of Ziph on the hill of Hachilah, which is before Jeshimon. The Ziphite tattlers (1 Samuel 23:19) ran to Saul, informing him of the most recent location of the fugitive. Evidently Saul's attitude of repentance in 1 Samuel 24 had changed, for he selected three thousand chosen men and once again sought the "partridge in the mountains." Saul pitched camp near the hill of Hachilah while David sought refuge in the wilderness. After evaluating the situation, David returned to his camp and asked who would accompany him to Saul's camp. Abishai volunteered. This youth was one of the sons of Zeruiah, David's sister. He, along with Joab and Asahel, were therefore David's nephews (1 Chronicles 2:15,16). Stealthily creeping under the cover of darkness, David and Abishai found Saul asleep in the trench with his spear stuck in the ground. Abner, along with the other soldiers, also lay asleep. Abishai felt that God had set up this perfect trap for the destruction of the King and begged David for permission to slay Saul with only one blow from his own spear.

(52) *David refused because Saul was God's anointed. The fugitive undoubtedly knew that he could not found a successful dynasty with the blood of the King on his hands. Although David would not perform the act, how did he feel that God would take care of that matter of destroying Saul* (1 Samuel 26:9-10)?

Taking the spear and also Saul's cruse of water, David and Abishai crept back to their own camp.

(53) *Why did no one hear David and Abishai* (verse 12)?

(54) *After climbing to another hill with Abishai, David called to Abner and rebuked him for failure to properly guard the King. What was David's reasoning? What evidence of his presence did David produce* (verses 13-16)?

(55) *Notice the beautiful figurative language in verse 20.*

(56) *What sort of effect did David's merciful attitude have upon Saul* (1 Samuel 26:21-25)? *Do you think it was easy for Saul to admit that one day David would prevail?*

*(57) Compare Saul's attitude in this instance with the one in 1 Samuel 24.* (Note that David had returned good for evil. This undoubtedly prompted Saul's replies. How difficult indeed it is for the Christian to learn this basic principle: if we want to change the manner in which people treat us, we must alter our actions toward them.)

After this event David and Saul parted, never again to meet upon this earth. The King left to meet his doom. David waited for the time to assume the leadership of the kingdom.

## Gath (1 Samuel 27:1-4)

Some think that David felt there was no hope for reconciliation. Since he would not kill the Lord's anointed himself and evidently did not want civil war to divide the nation of Israel, David fled for safety to the Philistine territory. This time he, his men, and his family went to dwell with King Achish at Gath.

*(58) What unpleasant earlier event had occurred at Gath (1 Samuel 21:10-15)? Why do you suppose David selected Gath, of all locations, as a place of refuge?*

## Ziklag (1 Samuel 27:5 - 28:2)

David persuaded Achish that it would be better if he and his people could have a village of their own in which to dwell. Therefore, the King of Gath gave Ziklag, located on the southern frontier of Judah near the border of Edom, to David as his very own town. The village originally had been given to the tribe of Judah (Joshua 15:31) and then to Simeon (Joshua 19:5 and 1 Chronicles 4:30). It was captured by the Philistines, but they never occupied the town. God's people were living there in subjection to the enemy. It became the home of David and his followers for a year and four months. At this point, David deceived Achish. The future heir to the throne of Israel was expected to conduct raids against his own people, but instead he spent most of his time fighting against the seminomadic enemies of Judah in the southern Negeb, such as the Geshurites, the Gezrites, and the Amalekites. Most of these were the original tribes which had inhabited Canaan. Saul had never destroyed them. Ruthless in his attacks, David left neither man nor woman alive lest they tell of his deeds. David thus strengthened the borders of his own people. Whenever Achish would ask David where he had fought that day, David deliberately lied, implying that he had wrought great havoc against his own people in the south of Judah. Achish believed David and was pleased: "He hath made his people Israel utterly to abhor him; therefore he shall be my servant forever."

(59) *What possible justification could you give for David's obvious deceit of Achish in killing the colleagues of the King of Gath and then deliberately lying about the matter by telling Achish that he had killed someone else* (verse 10)? *How do you suppose God felt about this deceit? Does the end ever justify the means?*

(60) *Note that David was strengthening his image in the eyes of his own people by such raids.*

When the Philistines readied themselves to fight Israel, Achish (the Philistine vassal king who was in a coalition army with five Philistine overlords in the north) remarked: "Know assuredly, that thou shalt go out with me to battle, thou and thy men" (1 Samuel 28:1). David could have been evading the issue when he said: "Surely thou shalt know what thy servant can do" (28:2). Nevertheless, Achish interpreted the answer as a favorable one for he made David "keeper of his head" forever.

(61) *Do you feel that David would have actually fought against his own people in this battle - the people over whom God had anointed to be their future king?*

### Shunem, Gilboa and Endor (1 Samuel 28:3-29:11)

Perhaps the death of Israel's spiritual leader Samuel (recorded in verse 3) precipitated the Philistine's decision to make a major attack at this time. The action changes from southern Judah to northern Israel as the next event of the narrative unfolds. We leave David waiting at Ziklag and move to the general vicinity of the plain of Esdraelon in northern Israel. Three famous mountains rear their heads from the floor of this beautiful valley: Tabor, Gilboa, and Moreh. Saul's men had pitched on the slopes of Mount Gilboa while the Philistine forces had converged across the valley near Shunem at the foot of Mt. Moreh. What a mighty confrontation that must have been! In fact, Saul was so afraid that his heart greatly trembled (verse 5). This sounds like a far cry from the leader who challenged his people to follow him to battle against the Ammonites when they had threatened the inhabitants of Jabesh-Gilead. (See 1 Samuel 11.) Wanting some sort of assurance of God's assistance, the King inquired of the Lord but He answered him not, neither by dreams nor by Urim.

(62) *What was Urim?* (See Numbers 27:21, Exodus 28:30, and Leviticus 8:8 in addition to a Bible encyclopedia.)

(63) *Why do you suppose God refused to answer Saul?*

Exasperated, Saul inquired where he could find a woman with an evil spirit in order that he might learn what the future held. This step seemed ironical since Saul had put familiar spirits and wizards out of the land (verses 3 and 9). This previous action of Saul was based upon two Biblical commands.

(64) *Read Leviticus 20:27 and Deuteronomy 18:10-11 for the direct commands for such action from God.*

(65) *By what power was the woman at Endor able to perform supernatural feats?* (In view of the two passages mentioned immediately above, could the power have come from God?)

Nothing is more exciting than the Word of God! The narration which unfolds from verses 8-25 is packed with action and suspense. Disguising himself with other clothes, Saul (accompanied by two other men) stealthily made his way to the other side of the mountain to meet this woman with supernatural powers.

(66) *On another sheet of paper, list the events of the evening in the order in which they happened.*

(67) *Was the woman aware that Saul's request was against the laws of the land* (verse 9)?

(68) *Why did the woman know Saul's true identity when Samuel was called forth* (verse 12)?

(69) *Describe Samuel* (verse 14).

(70) *Samuel stated that the Lord had departed from Saul and had become his enemy. When had this happened?* (Consider 1 Samuel 15:27-28. Note also 1 Samuel 28:18 in relationship to 1 Samuel 15:3-9.)

(71) *What was Saul's reaction* (verse 20)?

(72) *The woman at Endor went to considerably more trouble to show hospitality than modern women. What sort of preparation was necessary for the meal* (verse 24)?

(73) *As the Philistine lords gathered their forces in hundreds and thousands, what was their reaction to David and the other Israelites in the rear of the company with Achish* (1 Samuel 29:3-5)?

(74) *Do you feel that David was being completely honest in his reply to Achish* (1 Samuel 29:8)?

Acting upon the orders of Achish, David and his men arose early in the morning and returned to the town of Ziklag while the Philistines army readied for the battle.

## Ziklag (1 Samuel 20:1-31)

While Saul's army and the armies of the lords of the Philistines were gathering for battle in northern Israel, the Divine Author saw fit to take the reader back to Ziklag with David and his men to view a very exciting event which happened near David's adopted town. On the third day of the long journey from the northern part of Israel to the southern boundaries of Judah, Ziklag was invaded and burned by the Amalekites; and its inhabitants (families of David and his men) were carried away as captives. One of the most pathetic passages in the Scriptures is the fourth verse of this chapter: "Then David and the people that were with him lifted up their voices and wept, until they had no more power to weep." Even though David's two wives had been taken captive, the men spoke against David, apparently holding him responsible for this heartbreaking situation; "but David encouraged himself in the Lord his God" (verse 6).

(74) *David and his men had done essentially the same thing to the inhabitants of the bordering towns with one exception. Instead of taking captives, they had left no one alive to tell on them. In view of these actions, do you feel that these men had any reason for sorrow when they had been just as cruel as their enemies?*

(75) *Pause for just a moment and try to step into the shoes of Abigail, who had left a life of relative ease and financial security as the wife of the wealthy Nabal and who had now become one of two wives of this nomadic fugitive from the wrath of Saul as the former darted in and out of hiding places all over the land.*

Relying upon God's judgment, David requested the ephod from Abiathar the priest and asked God what to do. After receiving an affirmative answer, David and his six hundred set forth on this special mission. Two hundred became so faint that they could not go over the brook Besor. (In considering the reasons for their physical weakness, remember the ordeal of the arduous three day journey from northern Judah in addition to the emotional debilitation of discovering Ziklag pillaged.) After crossing the brook Besor, David and his company discovered an Egyptian from the band of invaders who had been abandoned without food or water because he had been too sick to keep up with the rest of the men. After being promised safety both

41

from David and his men and also his own people, the young man agreed to take David to the Amalekites. What a scene met their eyes! There the enemy was: "eating and drinking, and dancing, because of all the great spoil that they had taken out of the land of the Philistines, and of the land of Judah" (verse 16). From twilight until evening of the next day, David and his men smote the enemy until no one was left alive save the four hundred who fled on camels. (Remember that David only had four hundred men with him - the same number as the enemy which escaped. He must have been fighting against overwhelming odds.) Most fortunately, neither people nor possessions had been harmed so David recovered all in addition to the enemies' spoil from other towns.

(76) *When the men approached the two hundred who had been left behind at the brook Besor, what did the men who had just won the victory want to do* (verse 22)?

(77) *What was David's reply* (verses 23-25)? Note that this principle became the law of Israel from that day forward. Apply this philosophy to Christianity. Who are those today who "tarry by the stuff"?

(78) *To whom did David send presents of the spoil which he had taken* (verses 26-31)? *Why do you suppose he wanted to share with these people?*

### Gilboah (1 Samuel 31:1-13)

The reader is now mentally carried the three day journey back to the scene of the battle between Saul's men and the Philistines. When the narration is resumed, Saul is on the losing end of the struggle: "The men of Israel fled from before the Philistines, and fell down slain in mount Gilboah." Saul's three sons (Jonathan, Abinadab, and Melchishu) had already been killed when Saul was struck by an archer. Begging his armor bearer to put him out of his misery before the enemy abused him in his final hour, Saul's request was refused. In desperation Saul fell on his own sword. The armor bearer did likewise. Israelites from the surrounding towns forsook their dwelling places when they saw the hopelessness of the situation, and the Philistines took the towns over for their own. When the Philistines returned the next day to gather the spoil, they found Saul and his three sons dead on Mount Gilboa. Cutting off Saul's head and stripping him of his armor, the enemy sent the King's head into the land of the Philistines to confirm the victorious news.

(79) *What did they do with Saul's body and his armor* (verse 10)? Note also 1 Chronicles 10:10. *Do you recall what David did with Goliath's head?*

(80) *Who rescued the bodies of Saul and his sons from Bethshan* (verse 11)? *What did they do with the bodies* (verses 12-13)?

"So Saul died for his transgression which he committed against the Lord, even against the word of the Lord, which he kept not, and also for asking counsel of one that had a familiar spirit, to inquire of it, and inquired not of the Lord: therefore he slew him, and turned the kingdom unto David the son of Jesse" (1 Chronicles 10:13,14).

## Ziklag (2 Samuel 1:1-27)

When David had been back in Ziklag for two days (after going over the events which had transpired since David had left, try to estimate how many days probably elapsed), there must have been great excitement in David's town as a man came running into the camp with his clothes torn and dirt on his head. The stranger was the bearer of the tragic news of the death of Saul and his sons.

(82) *Read 2 Samuel 1:4-10 and compare the Amalekite's story with 1 Samuel 31:1-6. In what points do the two stories differ? What proof did the man have to offer?* (See verse 10.)

(83) *What do you think could have been the motive for such a lie? Could it have been the truth?*

David was so overcome with grief that he rent his clothes, mourned, wept, and fasted until even for Saul, Jonathan, and the whole nation of Israel for the deplorable condition in which they found themselves.

(84) *What was David's action against the messenger? What was the reason?* (See 2 Samuel 1:14-16.) *Did David evidently believe the story of the young man? Do you feel that David's action was justified? How could David have been so upset over an event which made the fulfillment of God's promise to the shepherd boy possible?*

(85) *The song recorded in verses 19:27 was said to have been written in the book of Jasher. See Joshua 10:13 for another reference to the same book.*

Thus ended the long reign of the first king of Israel - in disgrace and shame. In looking back over the events which had transpired, the reader may see the degradation of God's first anointed king as he fell from the height of achievement to the final decline which ended in a disgraceful death!

At the outset the young man's physical appearance demanded respect from the people. He was obedient to his father in addition to being genuinely humble. Self-confidence began to flow through the new king's veins as he asserted his leadership in gathering soldiers to meet an emergency. Power can be devastating. Saul's first disobedience is recorded as he took matters into his own hands in offering the sacrifice himself instead of waiting for Samuel. The same intoxicating power prompted his poor judgment in forbidding food to his people and even in his desire to have his own son slain for unknowingly tasting honey. Just as Saul felt powerful enough to take matters into his own hands regarding the sacrifice, so did he see fit to disobey God in failing to destroy King Agag. From the apex of power, Saul began his descent into the depth of despair. From the time the evil spirit from the Lord troubled him, Saul began to exhibit mental instability when the claws of jealousy wrapped themselves around him as David grew in favor with the people, thus posing a threat to the throne. This insecurity found tangible expression as Saul repeatedly tried to pin the lad to the palace wall with a javelin. Jonathan was even the victim of his father's wrath. Saul behaved more like a pouting child than a ruler when none felt sorry for him. The King deserted national affairs as the consuming passion to kill David prompted his constant searching for the future heir to the throne. Yet Saul responded in like manner to David's goodness and generosity when the young man refused to take advantage of killing God's anointed even when the task could have been performed so easily. Realizing that David would soon fulfill God's promise to replace Saul with another leader, the King was literally scared to death in his final battle with the Philistines. Even his death was shrouded with shame. Someone has stated that if the true test of a person's character is desired, just give him power. How true. How true.

## An Analysis of David's Characteristics at This Time

During the first part of this study, nearly all of David's actions were above reproach. His character was virtually flawless. During the approximate ten years of flight, however, the observant reader begins to detect both good and evil traits in the character of God's chosen one.

*Weaknesses* - David was *untruthful* to Ahimelech the priest at Nob by saying that Saul had sent him on a secret mission. Fear for his own life prompted God's anointed to act out a lie through deceit and hypocrisy before Achish, the king of Gath. Later David deliberately lied to this same king by telling the ruler that God's people instead of

Israel's enemies had been killed in the raids which originated from Ziklag.

Although the desire never reached fruition, David planned to *slaughter* Nabal and his men in retaliation for Nabal's rejection of David's plea for food. (This is more understandable as one remembers David's courteous treatment of Nabal's shearers when they were in the fields together.) Only Abigail's skillful diplomacy prevented the execution of this plot.

Of course the Amalekites had certainly done wrong in burning Ziklag and capturing its inhabitants, but *excessive vengeance* is implied in the statement that David "smote them from the twilight even unto the evening of the next day."

Also, *reckless abandon in killing* is also seen in the slaying of the young man who falsely claimed that he had killed King Saul.

Even though the practice of having *more than one wife* was becoming more prevalent, there was still no justification for this under the Law of Moses. The second phase of David's life closes with his having three wives.

*Strengths* - David was only human. Although he had some flaws in his character, the good traits far outnumbered the bad ones. David's good reputation for *bravery* preceded his escape to Gath. It was at this dangerous place that he displayed a trust in God in spite of overwhelming danger (Psalms 56).

Although many pressing problems must have been preying upon his mind, David placed his parents in a safe place while in exile. This same sense of *compassion* is seen in allowing those who were in trouble to follow him.

When the news of the destruction of the priests reached David's ears, he assumed the *responsibility* for the act.

David was willing to aid the inhabitants of Keilah when they were in distress but the young man relied heavily upon God's advice concerning the probability of Saul's victory. This same *spirit of kindness* is evidenced in the nomadic leader's almost tender treatment of the abandoned Egyptian while pursuing the Amalekites who had burned his town of Ziklag.

The future king showed a *sense of fairness* in the rebuking of his men for selfishly refusing to share the spoil of the Amalekites with the others who had waited at the brook Besor. God's anointed even shared with his own people who lived in nearby villages. Perhaps it was David's own sense of fairness which prompted his contempt for Nabal in an earlier event.

Regardless of how much Saul mistreated David, the youth had the utmost *respect for God's chosen one* by refusing to kill Saul when he was vulnerable in the cave of Engedi and also at the encampment in the wilderness of Ziph.

Ten years of being *hunted as a partridge* throughout the land must have been a mighty test of David's trust in God's promises. (So many of the Psalms echo a mixture of both the future king's *despair* and also his *trust* in God.)

Although David was a free moral agent who frequently made wrong choices as well as wise ones, the reader can see God's providential hands shaping the character of Israel's most beloved king. In addition to testing his faith and developing a deep reliance upon God, those years of exile physically toughened the next ruler of God's people. So often our response to God's promise is "I want it right now, God! Right now!" Yet, His reply to us may very well be: "It is not yet time, my child. Although you are not deserving now, the vicissitudes of life will gradually mold your character into one deserving of the responsibility."

David had successfully passed the ten years of testing and was now ready to face all the struggles involved in assuming the leadership of a great nation.

I had fainted, unless I had believed to see the goodness of the Lord in the land of the living. Wait on the Lord: be of good courage, and he shall strengthen thine heart: wait, I say, on the Lord.

Psalms 27:13,14

Part III

# After That The Full Corn In The Ear

## (2 Samuel 2:1 - 1 Kings 2:11)

I. David's Reign Over Judah
  A.  Recognition as King of Judah (2 Samuel 2:1-11)
  B.  Skirmish by the pool of Gibeon (2 Samuel 2:12-32 - 3:5)
  C.  Quarrel between Abner and Ishbosheth (2 Samuel 3:6-16)
  D.  Abner's negotiations with David (2 Samuel 3:17-21)
  E.  Abner killed by Joab (2 Samuel 3:22 - 4:39)
  F.  Assassination of Ishbosheth (2 Samuel 4:1-12)

II. David's Early Years As Ruler Of The Entire Kingdom
  A.  Anointed King over all Israel (2 Samuel 5:1-15)
  B.  Capture of Jerusalem (2 Samuel 5:6-16)
  C.  Philistines defeated by David (2 Samuel 5:17-25)
  D.  Ark brought to Jerusalem (2 Samuel 6:1-23)
  E.  David denied the right to build the temple (2 Samuel 7:1-29)

III. Period Of Foreign Conquests
  A.  Analysis of David's strategies (2 Samuel 8:1-14)
  B.  Key men of David's government (2 Samuel 8:15-18)
  C.  David's kindness to Mephibosheth (2 Samuel 9:1-13)
  D.  Defeat of the Ammonites and the Syrians (2 Samuel 10:1-19)
  E.  David and Bathsheba (2 Samuel 11:1-27)
  F.  David rebuked by Nathan (2 Samuel 12:1-25)
  G.  Rabbah captured (1 Samuel 12:26-31)

IV. Troublesome Latter Years
  A.  Absalom's reaction to Amnon and Tamar (2 Samuel 13:1-39)

B.  Joab's scheme for Absalom's return (2 Samuel 14:1-27)
C.  Absalom's plot to see his father (2 Samuel 14:28-33)
D.  The beginning of Absalom's revolt (2 Samuel 15:1-12)
E.  David's flight from Jerusalem (2 Samuel 15:13 - 16:14)
F.  Absalom as leader in Jerusalem (2 Samuel 16:15 - 17:23)
G.  The battle (2 Samuel 17:24 - 18:31)
H.  David's return to Jerusalem (2 Samuel 19:1-43)
I.  The revolt of Sheba (2 Samuel 20:1-26)
J.  The avenging of the Gibeonites (2 Samuel 21:1-4)
K.  David's last battle with the Philistines (2 Samuel
    21:15-22)
L.  David's song of deliverance (2 Samuel 22:1-51)
M.  David's mighty men (2 Samuel 23:8-39)
N.  Numbering of the people (2 Samuel 24:1-25)
O.  Abishag's services to the King (1 Kings 1:1-4)
P.  Adonijah's efforts to usurp the throne (1 Kings 1:5-53)
Q.  David's death (1 Kings 2:1-11)

48

# David's Early Reign

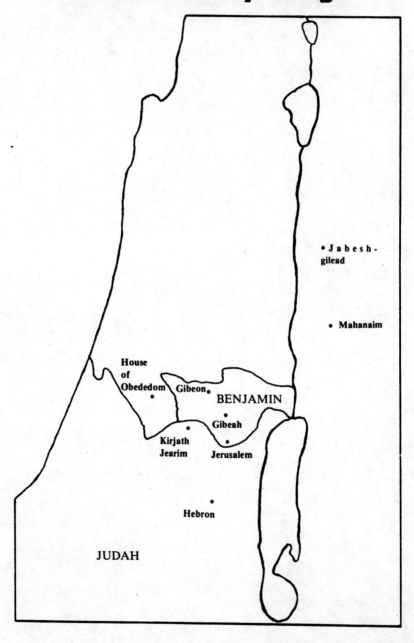

- •Jabesh-gilead
- • Mahanaim
- House of Obededom
- Gibeon•
- BENJAMIN
- Gibeah
- Kirjath Jearim
- Jerusalem
- Hebron
- JUDAH

Part III

# After That The Full Corn In The Ear

### David's Reign Over Judah

Saul's reign was over - ended in disgrace. Jonathan, David's closest earthly friend, was dead. In spite of the evil manner with which Saul had treated David, the former shepherd's sorrow seemed to be genuine. Such an attitude was not human. It would have been impossible without a proper respect for God's wishes and also for God's anointed one, regardless of how evil that one might be.

After a short time of fasting, mourning, and seeking God's desire in the matter, David moved his troops and family to the town of Hebron, where the male leaders proclaimed him to be the new king over Judah. (The time was approximately 1000 B.C. and David was thirty years old.) Note that this was the second anointing. The first was done privately (1 Samuel 16:12,13). Although Saul had reigned over a united kingdom, the upper portion still had strong ties of loyalty with the former king. Those faithful to the house of Saul (headed by Abner, captain of the army) declared his forty year old son Ishbosheth as king. Thus, the fulfillment of God's promise to Jesse's son began with David's ruling over a divided, still warring nation for seven and a half years.

(1) *Try to step into David's shoes and ask whether or not you would have possessed the patience to wait seventeen and a half years to have a promise completely fulfilled.*

### Skirmish By The Pool Of Gibeon

(2 Samuel 2:12-32 - 3:5) - The leaders of the two opposing forces (Abner and Joab, David's nephew) gathered by the pool of Gibeon (a little north of Jerusalem) for a skirmish. Twelve men from each side were selected to engage in a type of tournament to determine the victors. The result was a tie with all twenty-four men dead. A real battle followed. This time David's men prevailed. Evidently Abner realized

that he had lost because he began running with Joab's brother, Asahel, close behind.

(2) *How fast was Asahel* (2 Samuel 2:18)?

(3) *How was Asahel killed* (2 Samuel 2:23)?

David not only lost a faithful soldier, but Asahel's death later precipitated a blood feud between Joab and Abner. Joab and his other brother, Abishai, would not let Abner rest. Continuing the race until sundown, Abner and his forces called to Joab and his men from the top of a hill. After Abner had pointed out the foolishness of such killings between brethren, Joab agreed, admitting that neither had his side desired such and would have returned home by daylight anyway. Joab officially ended the conflict by blowing a trumpet and both sides spent the night walking back home. The final battle toll clearly indicated, however, that David's men had been victorious. Sporadic civil war in the years to come favored David's forces.

During the internal strife, David continued to make his headquarters at Hebron. It was here that six sons were born to him.

(4) *List the sons and their mothers* (2 Samuel 3:2-5).

(5) *How many more wives had David acquired?*

## Quarrel Between Abner and Ishbosheth

(2 Samuel 3:6-16) - While David's power was growing stronger, trouble developed between Abner and Ishbosheth when Abner took Rizpah, Saul's concubine. The taking of what was considered to be royal property greatly angered Ishbosheth. After sharp words, Abner prepared to shift his loyalty to David.

Before David would talk with Abner, however, the King demanded the return of his first wife - Michal - who had been given to Phaltiel.

(6) *Do you feel that David's desire for Michal was based upon love or upon a desire to have his position strengthened by having Saul's daughter as his wife? State your reasons.*

(7) *Try to place yourself in the shoes of Phaltiel as he weepingly followed Michal* (2 Samuel 3:15-16).

## Abner's Negotiations With David

(2 Samuel 3:17-21) - It was upon Abner's advice that the northern kingdom agreed to accept David as the King. After this diplomacy Abner went to David with the good news. David agreed and Abner started back home with the glad tidings.

### Abner Killed By Joab

(2 Samuel 3:22-4:39) - When Joab returned from battle and discovered that Abner had not only been in Hebron but had also been sent away in peace, David's captain was greatly angered. Secretly a messenger was sent for Abner. Joab, along with his brother Abishai, stabbed Saul's leader under the fifth rib by the gate at Hebron, thus seeking revenge for the death of their brother Asahel. Such action would naturally have provoked bitterness among the northern tribes. David acted wisely, however, in letting it be known that he had no part in the murder by ordering a state funeral, walking behind the bier while weeping and fasting all day. Such action pleased the people.

(8) *Do you feel that Joab could ever have worked successfully with Abner, his rival commander, in a merger of the two kingdoms? State your reasons.*

### The Assassination of Ishbosheth

(2 Samuel 4:1-12) - Shortly after the death of Abner, Ishbosheth was murdered in his bed by two rival leaders of the army - Rechab and Baanah. Bringing the head to Hebron, they thought they would find favor in David's sight. Instead of a reward, the two men were put to death. Their hands and feet were cut off and hung over the pool in Hebron as a public spectacle.

(9) *How can you account for such gruesome actions as the cutting off of a head, hands and feet?*

(10) *Note verse 4 of this chapter. What was the reason for the lameness of Mephibosheth, son of Jonathan?*

### David's Early Years As King Of The Entire Kingdom
### David Anointed King Over All Israel

(2 Samuel 5:1-5) - With the slaying of Ishbosheth, there were no more sons of Saul alive and David was free to assume the leadership of the entire kingdom. The elders of the northern kingdom went to Hebron to anoint the new ruler. (Note that this was the third anointing.)

(11) *What reasons did they give for accepting David as their ruler* (2 Samuel 5:1-3)?

(12) *From verses 4 and 5 tell how many years David ruled over each part of the kingdom.*

(13) *How old did this make David when he died?*

It had been a long time since Samuel had made his visit to

Bethlehem to anoint Jesse's youngest son as king. At that time David was only a lad. During his teen years the shepherd boy divided his time between Saul's court and his duties with his flock. Gradually he spent more and more time at the house of Saul until forced to flee for his own safety. For approximately ten years the lad who had grown into young manhood led a nomadic existence darting in and out of every conceivable hiding place as Saul sought him as a partridge. After the death of the King and David's anointing as ruler over Judah at Hebron, it was yet another seven and a half years before the third and final anointing publicly proclaimed David as Saul's successor. Try to imagine David's feelings during all these years!

## Capture of Jerusalem

(2 Samuel 5:6-17) - The anointing of David as king over both the northern and southern parts of the kingdom necessitated the selection of a suitable capital. Jerusalem, the last city still controlled by the Canaanites in central Israel, was neutral ground and situated ideally on the border between Judah and Israel. Built on a high ridge and bordered on the east, west, and south by steep valleys, it seemed to be the logical capital for David's rule.

Jerusalem is mentioned in the Scriptures several times before this incident. Melchizedek was the king of Salem, so the town was known even in Abraham's time. Reference is also made in Joshua 10:1,3. When the land was divided among the tribes, Jerusalem fell to Benjamin's lot (Joshua 18:28); but the children of Benjamin allowed the Canaanite Jebusites to continue living there (Judges 1:21) until it became known as a city of Jebusites.

When David prepared to attack the city, he was mocked by its inhabitants, the Jebusites. Jeering from the top of the walls, the defenders of the city mocked David who offered the reward of being the chief leader of his army to the one who would smite the Jebusites first. The Scriptures are not specific, but evidently Joab led some of the men through a water tunnel (a concealed passageway cut through the rock under the city that ran from the spring Gihon in the eastern valley to a place inside the walls) and attacked the Jebusites from the rear. The victory was complete. Now David had his own personal city, being occupied neither by Judah nor Israel, from which he could rule God's people. "Nevertheless, David took the castle of Zion, which is the city of David . . . And David dwelt in the castle . . . And he built the city round about, even from Milo round about: and Joab repaired the rest of the city" (1 Chronicles 11:5-8). Some Bible scholars believe

54

that Milo was a townhall or place for public gatherings. Beginning with the castle and Milo, David enlarged the city for his capital.

While Saul had held the tribes together in a loose confederacy, David centralized the power in the throne of the king with Jerusalem as the seat of government. After so many years, David was now the uncontested ruler.

(14) *Who sent the materials and labor to build David a house in the capital* (2 Samuel 5:11)? Note the increase of David's family in verses 13-16.

## Philistines Defeated By David

(2 Samuel 5:17-25) - Naturally the Philistines were alarmed by this new threat to their power. Gathering in the valley of Rephaim southwest of Jerusalem, David defeated Israel's longtime foes - not once but twice! (Note the verses to determine the two different strategies.) After at least two more skirmishes, the Philistine armies were destroyed and would never again pose a threat to Israel.

(15) *Read 1 Chronicles 11:15-19 to learn what happened during one of these battles when David desired water from the well at Bethlehem. What is your opinion of his attitude?*

## Ark Brought To Jerusalem

(2 Samuel 6:1-23) - Jerusalem was destined not only to be the capital of David's empire. He also wanted it to be the center of Israel's religious world. Such a desire necessitated the moving of the ark of God from the house of Abinadab at Gibeah.

(16) *For how many years had the ark been at this place* (1 Samuel 7:1-2)?

(17) *What were the circumstances under which the ark was placed at this location* (1 Samuel 5,6)?

The ark had always been sacred. It was from between the two cherubim on the ark that Jehovah had promised to commune with his people (Exodus 25:21,22). It was this sacred object that was carried around the walls of Jericho. Later the ark was carried into battle as a mascot. When the Philistines captured it, they carried Israel's sacred belonging in triumph through their cities and even placed it in the temple of Dagon. Later Jehovah had the ark sent back where it was welcomed by the inhabitants of Bethshemesh. When they looked within the holy chest, the Lord smote them with a great slaughter (1 Samuel 6:19).

After this incident the ark was moved to Kerjathjearim, a village of the woods, and placed in the house of Abinadab. Here for over fifty years the ark was forgotten. During the days of Saul, they "inquired not at it" (1 Chronicles 13:3). Even in David's youth this neglect bothered the lad. He vowed to find a habitation for the ark in the fields of the wood (Psalms 132:1-7).

The moving of the ark must have been a momentous occasion, for David took thirty thousand of his chosen men to accompany the journey of God's sacred dwelling place. Can you imagine such an entourage? Jehovah's Word had been explicit. The ark was supposed to be covered, staves were to be inserted in the rings, and it was to be carried on the shoulders of the Kohathites (Numbers 4:5,6; Numbers 4:15, and Numbers 7:9). Not only did David fail to have the ark carried by staves on the shoulders of designated men, he even had it placed on a cart - a new cart! (Note that David's ignoring of the command in Deuteronomy 17:18,19 could have been responsible for his ignorance.)

Abinadab's two sons (Uzzah and Ahio) walked beside the ark as it made its journey to Jerusalem. When the men reached Nachon's threshing floor, Uzzah made a great mistake. The ark, shaken by the oxen, appeared to be falling. Obeying natural instincts instead of intellect, Uzzah impulsively steadied the ark with his hand. Although this was a well meant, kind act, it was disobedience to God's commands and Uzzah was struck dead immediately.

(18) *Try to step into Uzzah's shoes. Imagine growing up with something as sacred as the ark of God in your father's house. Then try to visualize Uzzah's terror as he saw the ark tremble. What would your reaction have been under such circumstances?*

This episode so frightened David that he would not continue the ark's transfer to Jerusalem. Instead, it was taken to the house of Obededom for three months. Since Obededom was blessed by God, David must have interpreted this as a sign that it was now time to bring the ark into the capital city. Caught up in the excitement of the trumpets, the huge crowds, and the sacrifices, David truly made a spectacle of himself as he lost the dignity of his office while leaping and dancing before the Lord, girded with a linen ephod. Although this was the clothing worn by priests when officiating, yet it was also worn by those who were not priests (1 Samuel 2:18). Such revelry must have inspired the King's impetuous generosity.

(19) *What did David give to each person* (2 Samuel 6:19)?

Michal (Saul's daughter and David's true wife) had observed David's undignified actions as she watched through a window. Instead of welcoming David with outstretched arms and sharing in his joy, Michal greeted her husband with better sarcasm and renunciation for his inappropriate actions. Her life was henceforth cursed with barrenness, a great disgrace in those days.

(20) *Review the events which transpired in Michal's life* (1 Samuel 18:20-30; 1 Samuel 19:11-17; 2 Samuel 3:12-16). *Do you feel that there was ever genuine love between David and his wife?*

## David Denied The Right To Build The Temple

(2 Samuel 7:1-27) - After many years of waiting, David's dreams had at long last come true. He was the ruler of the kingdom - both parts. The ark had been brought into the city of Jerusalem, thus centralizing both the government and spiritual realms of the kingdom.

David had built for himself a royal palace. It seemed inappropriate for the ark of God not to have a suitable dwelling place also. In gratitude for all Jehovah's blessings David, wanting to build a magnificent edifice, sought the advice of Nathan, the prophet. Through this man of God, David was informed that the privilege would not be his. Instead the Almighty would build a house for David.

(21) *What was to be the nature of this "house"* (2 Samuel 7:11-17)?

(22) *What reason was given for the denial to build the Temple* (1 Chronicles 22:8-10)?

## David's Foreign Conquests

David's achievements had been spectacular. After many long years of waiting and struggling, the kingdom had at last been united. Now the time had come for Israel to become the mighty nation promised to Abraham.

Since the southern and western borders were no longer threatened after the defeat of the Philistines, David seized upon the favorable conditions and launched a series of wars of expansion. The political weakness of the major world powers made this an opportune time. For a number of years Babylonia had been on the decline. The Hurrians had been destroyed by the Hittites and Assyrians. Since that time the Hittites had lost their power. Egypt's leaders were too weak to pose a threat to Israel.

# David's Conquests

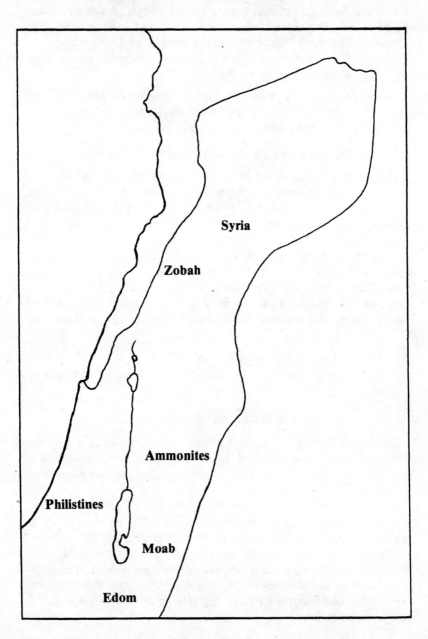

Syria

Zobah

Ammonites

Philistines

Moab

Edom

Closer to home (to the east), David quickly smote the Moabites, who were the descendants of Lot. (Moab is my washpot - Psalms 60:8). In the north and northeast the Syrians were eventually brought under control. The Edomites had been a threat in the south and southeast for years, but they also came under the rule of Israel. (Psalms 60:8 states: "Over Edom will I cast out my shoe." It has been said that this was an eastern symbol of claiming a slave.) A short time later the Ammonites were defeated in the battle which so tragically involved Bathsheba's husband.

Thus, for the first time since God's covenant with Abraham in Genesis 15:18, God's people possessed what had been promised to them. Now they controlled the land from the wilderness of Sinai to the Euphrates and from the Arabian Desert to the Mediterranean Sea, an area at least five times as large as that conquered by the twelve tribes. The conquest of Edom gave Israel control over the copper mines. The western victories to the Gulf of Aqaba and the Red Sea later gave Israel a potential port. Under Solomon the nation would trade from there with Arabia and Africa. The conquest of eastern Syria gave Israel control of the trade routes to the Euphrates River.

## An Analysis Of David's Strategies

David did not go into these battles blindly. Well prepared plans and trust in God were the underlying factors behind all the victories. Twice in the eighth chapter of 2 Samuel the statement is made: "And the Lord preserved David whithersoever he went" (verses 6,14). Whatever David was doing, the strategies must have been pleasing in God's sight.

First, King David, in refusing to rely upon the power of chariot horses (2 Samuel 8:4), was obeying the command given in Deuteronomy 17:15-16.

(22) *What was this command? Why do you suppose it was given?*

(23) *Also note Psalms 20:7 and Psalms 33:17.*

Second, David had the foresight to capture valuable items from his enemies.

(24) *Scan the eighth chapter of 2 Samuel and make a list of the things confiscated. Was there anything morally wrong in seizing these possessions?*

(25) *Do you suppose these riches were used in the building of Solomon's magnificent temple? (Note 1 Chronicles 18.)*

Third, David was able humbly to accept all the praise heaped upon him: "And David was given a name when he returned from smiting of the Syrians . . . " (2 Samuel 8:13). Just as in earlier days at King Saul's court when David was lauded for his conquests in battle (1 Samuel 18:7), Jehovah's anointed was able to keep his values in proper perspective.

Fourth, in spite of the achievements of his foreign conquests, David remembered one of his main obligations. He executed judgment and justice unto all his people (2 Samuel 8:15).

In summary we may conclude that in all of David's foreign conquests, he was able to put God first and rely upon Him instead of worldly security (horses, valuables, personal honor and fame) in addition to subduing the inclination to place conquests above the needs of his own people.

### Key Men In David's Government

(2 Samuel 8:16-18) - At this point the inspired writer paused long enough to name the men in the key places in David's government.

(26) *List these men:*

_____commander in chief

_____recorder (kept official records, probably arranged David's public appearances, and acted as mediator between David and the people)

_____and _____ the sons of Abiathar, who had served during the years of the exile (note the incident in 1 Samuel 22), were priests.

_____scribe or secretary, similar to a secretary of state, handled David's official correspondence.

_____David's personal bodyguard (over the Cherethites and the Pelethites, who had accompanied David in the wilderness)

_____Chief rulers

### David's Kindness To Mephibosheth

(2 Samuel 9:1-13) - In the midst of all David's foreign conquests, a seemingly unimportant incident in the King's life is recorded in the Scriptures. It is a glimpse into the valleys of David's life such as this

60

that gives the reader an understanding of the true character of this man after God's own heart.

King David was the undisputed ruler of Israel. His foreign conquests had enlarged the kingdom as never before. In the midst of all his glory, however, Jonathan's closest friend remembered a promise that had been made years ago.

(27) *What was the promise made in 1 Samuel 20:14-17?*

(28) *Discuss the last known meeting between these two friends* (1 Samuel 23:15-18).

Ziba, a former servant of Saul, was called before the King for questioning regarding any living heirs to Saul's family for Jonathan's sake. In an earlier chapter (2 Samuel 4:4) a very simple - but dramatic - statement was made concerning an accident involving Jonathan's son, Mephibosheth. When news of the deaths of Saul and Jonathan reached home, evidently Mephibosheth's nurse must have feared for the safety of Jonathan's son, for she dropped the young lad in her haste to flee. The accident resulted in the lameness of the boy. Nothing more is mentioned in the Scriptures until this incident. Evidently a number of years must have passed because Mephibosheth now had a son of his own. He was found living in the land of Lodebar, commonly called "the barren place." Apparently the young prince had been living in a self-imposed exile for fear of his own life.

(29) *From this passage select statements which depict Mephibosheth's fear for his safety.*

(30) *What was David's decision regarding the treatment of Jonathan's son* (2 Samuel 9:9-13)?

(31) *Why do you suppose Ziba, his sons, and his servants were placed in such a servile position?*

(32) *For a preview of another encounter with Mephibosheth, read 2 Samuel 19:24-30.*

### Defeat Of The Ammonites and the Syrians

(2 Samuel 10:1-19) - In the midst of the accounts of David's foreign conquests, the reader is permitted to enter a seldom noticed valley of David's life for an interesting account of the defeat of the Ammonites. Hanun ruled these people after his father's death. It seems that in earlier years the older king had shown kindness to David. In an effort to show gratitude David sent servants to comfort the bereaved. Instead of accepting this act as a good-will gesture, Hanun listened to

the princes' opinion that these men were spies. Their treatment was most humiliating.

(33) *Read 2 Samuel 10:4-5 to discover the manner in which they were received.*

(34) *What was David's reaction* (2 Samuel 10:6)? Note this same expression used in Genesis 34:30.

The Ammonites enlisted the aid of the Syrians with their chariots. Joab divided Israel's forces into two companies, placing half under the leadership of his brother Abishai.

(35) *Compare the tenth chapter of 2 Samuel with the nineteenth chapter of 1 Chronicles to determine the outcome of the battle.*

### David And Bathsheba

(2 Samuel 11:1-27) - The Syrians seem to have been subdued, but the Ammonites were not yet completely conquered. David sent Joab and the soldiers to defeat one of these last remaining enemies of Israel. (By this time in David's life his kingdom had been so firmly established that the King could either choose to battle personally or remain in Jerusalem and send his men under Joab. This time David should have gone into battle!) Jerusalem's weather can be stifling during the hot, dry season. David could not sleep, so he took a seemingly harmless walk on his roof. That's when the trouble started. The King certainly was not perfect and had made his mistakes, but the adultery and murder involved in this episode seemed to have been the turning point in David's life. After this time, trouble plagued David for the remainder of his years.

Roofs of homes were used in a different sense during this period of history. They served as another sitting room from which the inhabitants could escape the heat of the city. We are not told why Bathsheba chose this particular spot for her bath. The reason for her bathing is given in verse four. (She was purified from her uncleanness.)

(36) *For further study of this ceremonial cleansing, read Leviticus 15:19-30 and Leviticus 18:19.*

Lust prompted David's decision to send for this beautiful young woman. Messengers brought her to the King's palace where adultery was committed. After a due course of time Bathsheba sent word to David that she was with his child.

As usual, it is extremely difficult to cover one sin with another. In

God's sight David was already guilty of adultery, for Jehovah had only intended one husband and one wife from the beginning. Before David assumed the leadership of the southern part of the kingdom at Hebron, he had already taken two wives in addition to his original one. Gradually he kept adding to the number in addition to his concubines. But this case was different in the eyes of his subjects. The King had not just taken a lovely young maiden into his court. He had taken a woman who was already married to Uriah the Hittite, a soldier in Israel's army.

David thought he could cover his sin by sending for Uriah with the anticipation that the young soldier would naturally visit his own wife while he was in Jerusalem. Not so with Uriah! His devotion to Israel's army was so strong that this loyalty took precedence over any natural desires.

After small talk concerning the progress of the war, David suggested that Uriah go to his home and freshen up. The King even sent a mess of meat with the weary soldier!

(37) *What reason did Uriah give for refusing to go home* (2 Samuel 11:11)?

(38) *What was David's next line of strategy? Did it work?* (See 2 Samuel 11:13).

(39) *Out of desperation David devised a cruel manner in which to have Uriah killed. Read 2 Samuel 11:14-25 and describe the scheme.* (Note that Rabbah was the location of the modern city of Amman.)

(40) *Was there any way in which this third plan could have freed David from guilt in the eyes of his people?*

## David Rebuked By Nathan

(2 Samuel 12:1-25) - David had committed a terrible series of sins. Not only was he guilty of adultery. To that sin he had added lies, hypocrisy, and even murder. Most assuredly, this incident was the turning point in David's life. Although the King's life had not been without wrongs, still his heart seemed right and he was traveling in a direction that was pleasing to God as His ruler. From this moment on, David's life was one heartache after another - both from within and without.

There was no doubt about it. David had done wrong. He had sinned. Either he was unaware of his shortcomings (which is a little difficult to believe) or else his heart had become so hardened that he would not admit his sins even to himself. Regardless of his motives,

63

wrong had to be rebuked. This difficult task fell upon the shoulders of Nathan, God's spokesman. Quite frankly, I would have dreaded standing in Nathan's shoes. By this time (nearly a year later) everyone in the kingdom must have known what David had done. As head of the kingdom, David could easily have taken Nathan's life; but something had to be done in the name of righteousness. Instead of pompously rebuking the King, Nathan chose the strategy of a parable.

True to Nathan's prophecy, the son of David and Bathsheba died when he was only seven days old. (Note that the Israelite males were to be circumcised on the eighth day. This child died before he could even receive the sign of the covenant which God had made with His people.) Distraught with grief, David had neither eaten nor slept during the baby's illness. When the infant actually died, the servants dreaded telling the King since he had already been so mournful.

(41) *Relate the main events in the parable* (2 Samuel 12:1-4).

(42) *What was David's reaction* (2 Samuel 12:5,6)?

(43) *Discuss the skill required to maneuver David into passing his own sentence.*

(44) *Discuss the impact of Nathan's statement: "Thou art the man."*

(45) *List all the things which Nathan had previously done for David* (2 Samuel 12:7,8).

(46) *Keep in mind the statement: "Now therefore the sword shall never depart from thine house . . ." in the chapters which follow.*

(47) *Read the fulfillment of the prophecy in verses 11 and 12 in 2 Samuel 16:22.*

(48) *David confessed his sin (verse 13). Why was David to be punished by the death of his innocent son (2 Samuel 12:14)?*

(49) *What was David's surprised reaction (2 Samuel 12:20-23)? What does verse twenty-three prompt the reader to think of David's views of life after death?*

(50) *What good came from all this sorrow and tribulation* (2 Samuel 12:24,25)? *What other sons were born to David and Bathsheba* (1 Chronicles 3:5)?

The twelfth chapter of 2 Samuel primarily presents the facts. If the reader would like an insight into David's real feelings and emotions, turn to Psalms 51:

"Wash me, and I shall be whiter than snow. Make me to hear the joy and gladness; that the bones which thou hast broken may rejoice."

## Rabbah Captured

(2 Samuel 12:26-31) - Although the defeat of the Ammonites had been a slow one, victory was imminent. Joab could easily have finished the task, but he respected his master and wanted King David to receive the glory. David assumed his rightful place as leader of the army and the matter was quickly settled. (If David had been leading his army instead of walking around on rooftops, he would have been spared much agony in the first place!)

The acquisition of Rabbah added the finishing touches to the expansion of David's earthly empire to that of a mighty one, but it heralded the decline of a peaceful kingdom and the beginning of much heartache and sorrow. "For whatsoever a man soweth, that shall he also reap" (Galatians 6:7).

## Troublesome Latter Years

Generally speaking, things had gone well with David. Before the incident with Bathsheba, David's patient waiting for God's promise had been rewarded with the largest kingdom God's people had ever known. Instead of a few scattered tribes, unskilled in fighting and lacking in riches, David had united the Israelites as no other leader had ever done before. External circumstances in the world favored the nation's growth at this time. As David made Israel a mighty force and endeared himself to the hearts of his people, all those years of darting in and out of the wilderness areas as the lad ran from the wrath of King Saul must have faded into oblivion.

After the incident with Bathsheba, however, it seemed that David's troubles increased both in quantity and intensity. In fact, there was no more real peace.

## Absalom's Reaction To Amnon and Tamar

(2 Samuel 13:1-39) - It seems that Tamar was the only daughter of David mentioned by name. Since she was the daughter of David and Maacah, who was the daughter of the king of Geshur, she and Absalom had the same mother and father. A half brother, Amnon (David's eldest son by Ahinoam and heir to the throne) found the virgin Tamar most attractive. (Do you remember the mention of Ahinoam after David's encounter with the beautiful Abigail? Many Bible scholars believe that David married Ahinoam before Abigail since the former's son is always listed first in any enumeration of David's sons. Anyway, Ahinoam faithfully followed David throughout his many years of wilderness wanderings.)

65

(51) *Jonadab, friend of Amnon and nephew to David, suggested a treacherous plan whereby Amnon might take sexual advantage of his half sister. What was this plan?* (See 2 Samuel 13:4-10.) *What were the results* (verses 11-14)? Note the violation of these Scriptures: Exodus 22:16-17; Deuteronomy 22:28-29; Leviticus 20:17; Leviticus 18:9,11; Deuteronomy 27:22.

(52) *After the physical conquest, "Amnon hated her exceedingly"* (verses 15). *Is this situation different from today's general opinion after sexual conquest? Discuss the implications for modern young people.*

(53) *Describe the pitiful turn of events* (2 Samuel 13:15-19).

(54) *Absalom took his sister into his own house after her disgrace. Why do you suppose that he advised her to remain silent* (2 Samuel 13:20)?

(55) *When King David learned of the happening, he was very angry; but he did nothing* (2 Samuel 13:21). *What are your opinions concerning David's reasoning?*

Absalom may have remained silent, but the incident was very much alive in his heart. After two full years an opportune time for revenge presented itself.

(56) *Give the details of Absalom's plan and the results* (2 Samuel 13:23-33).

(57) *Absalom fled. Review his lineage at the beginning of this incident and tell why you think Absalom escaped to Geshur.* (See 2 Samuel 3:3.) (With the death of Amnon and no further mention of Chileab, David's second son, Absalom became the obvious heir.)

(58) *In your opinion, did Absalom have Amnon killed because of revenge for Tamar or to secure legal rights to the throne?*

### Joab's Scheme For Absalom's Return

(2 Samuel 14:1-27) - Joab was always in the thick of things! Evidently he must have felt that David really wanted Absalom to return: "Now Joab . . . perceived that the king's heart was toward Absalom" (verse 1). In order to facilitate the homecoming, Joab devised a scheme with a wise woman of Tekoah.

(59) *In your own words, relate the story the woman told and David's reply. Up to this point, do you feel that this was an effective manner by which to convince David? Does this in any way remind you of Nathan's story concerning the lamb?* (Refer to 2 Samuel 12.)

66

(60) *Why do you suppose David suspicioned that Joab was behind this plot* (2 Samuel 14:18-20)?

(61) *2 Samuel 13:39 states: "David longed to go forth unto Absalom" when the latter fled to Geshur. Even though the King allowed his son to return, why did David refuse to see his own flesh and blood* (verse 24)? Note that this continued for two years!

(62) *After reading 2 Samuel 14:25-26, describe Absalom.* (Note that his hair would weigh over twelve pounds in our system of weights.)

## Absalom's Plot To See His Father

(2 Samuel 14:28-33) - Absalom had lived with his relatives in Geshur for three years. Joab's scheme enabled the young man to return to Jerusalem, but for two years the King refused to even look upon his son. Absalom turned to his friend Joab, who had been so instrumental in getting the fugitive back to Jerusalem. Twice Absalom sent for Joab. Twice Joab refused. In order to get his attention, Joab's field was ordered burned. That got results! Joab secured permission for Absalom to appear before David. After bowing to the ground, Absalom was kissed by his father.

(63) *Do you feel that the kiss was a sincere one?*

(64) *Compare Absalom's order to have Joab's field burned with the misbehavior of many disobedient children in order to gain attention.*

(65) *Absalom was on the verge of revolt. Scan back over the events of the previous seven years. If David's actions and attitudes had been different, do you feel that Absalom's rebellion could have been prevented? Relate this situation with modern problems between parents and children.* (Note that some Bible scholars relate Psalms 41 and Psalms 55 with this period of David's life. What is your opinion?)

## Absalom Begins His Revolt

(2 Samuel 15:1-12) - Evidently during the five years of rejection by David, Absalom had been plotting his revenge.

(66) *From verses 1-6 outline the manner in which Absalom stole the hearts of the men of Israel.* Note that the use of horses is a direct violation of Deuteronomy 17:16. Samuel had warned that the selection of kings as rulers would result in chariots and horsemen (1 Samuel 8:11). The choosing of fifty men to run before him was a symbol of royalty. Thus, Absalom feigned power by his appearance while at the same time he pretended to be genuinely interested in the problems of the people and undermined David's administration. The

kingdom was not destroyed from without. It disintegrated through the seeds of discontent and disloyalty which were planted by Absalom.)

Absalom gained permission to go to Hebron apparently to pay a vow he had made years before. Shrewd Absalom! He sent spies throughout all the land with instructions to proclaim him as King when they heard the trumpet. The young man's entourage even included two hundred unsuspecting men who knew nothing of the plot.

(67) *Absalom sent for Ahithophel the Gilonite. The man was David's counselor, similar to a prime minister. One cannot help but wonder why such a loyal and high ranking man would turn against David. Read 2 Samuel 11:3 and then 2 Samuel 23:34. Whose grandfather was Ahithophel? Do you feel that David's previous action against the man's granddaughter could have influenced Ahithophel's treason?*

### David's Flight From Jerusalem

(2 Samuel 15:13 - 16:14) - Poor David! The mighty ruler of the powerful nation of Israel had been brought to his knees in disgrace. As Absalom was preparing to overtake his father's kingdom, King David felt it best to flee the city for a number of reasons. Leaving behind ten of his concubines at the palace, David and several hundred of his loyal supporters fled from the city. Even Ittai the Gittite and his people followed the King. (Some think that this was the son of Achish, the King of Gath.) What a pitiful sight it must have been as David and his loyal friends walked out of Jerusalem and passed over the brook Kidron.

(68) *Why did David send the ark back to Jerusalem* (2 Samuel 15:25-26)?

(69) *Why did David send Zadok and Abiathar, the high priests, and their two sons back to Jerusalem with the ark* (2 Samuel 15:27-29)?

Leaving behind a few of his trusted friends to keep him informed of the developments in Jerusalem, King David left the beautiful Jerusalem in shame and disgrace: barefooted, weeping, and head covered as he made his way up the Mount of Olives. (Does this weeping king remind the reader of a spiritual king who later wept in agony on this very mount?) The servant Hushai also wanted to follow his master, but David felt it best to send him back to Jerusalem with Zadok and Abiathar, the high priests, and their sons to keep the King informed of the happenings there.

(70) *Ziba, the servant of Mephibosheth, brought David and his followers food along with the news that Mephibosheth (Jonathan's son) was waiting at Jerusalem to have the kingdom restored unto him* (2 Samuel 16:1-4). *Do you feel that this was really true?* (See 2 Samuel 19:24-29.)

(71) *What did Shimei, the son of Gera, do to David* (2 Samuel 16:5-8?) *What was David's attitude* (2 Samuel 16:9-14)?

## Absalom As Leader In Jerusalem

(2 Samuel 16:15 - 17:23) - When Absalom had triumphantly entered Jerusalem with Ahithophel, his chief advisor, and his other followers, he questioned the loyalty of Hushai, a secret representative of David. Evidently Hushai was successful in convincing Absalom of his trustworthiness.

(72) *What terrible act did Ahithophel advise Absalom to do* (2 Samuel 16:20-23)? Note 2 Samuel 12:11.

Ahithophel urged Absalom to attack David immediately with his 12,000 men before David could gather his loyal armies. Hushai, a former advisor of David who had sworn allegiance to Absalom but secretly remained loyal to David, urged Absalom to gather all the armies of Israel before the attack. (The motive behind this advice was to give David more time to cross the Jordan and to gather his forces.)

Hushai's advice influenced Absalom more than that of Ahithophel. Jonathan and Ahimaaz, sons of the priests whom David had sent back to Jerusalem, were sent on the dangerous mission of informing David of the impending attack.

(73) *Narrate the exciting details of this dangerous mission.* (See 2 Samuel 17:15-22.)

(74) *What happened to Ahithophel when he learned that his advice had been ignored* (2 Samuel 17:23)?

## The Battle

(1 Samuel 17:24 - 18:31) - Absalom and his forces (under the leadership of Amasa) gathered in the land of Gilead. Meanwhile, David was preparing in Mahanaim, where food and other supplies were brought to him by friends.

Hushai's stalling had given David time to organize his men. Dividing them into thirds, he placed one part under the direction of Joab, another under Abishai, and the third under Ittai the Gittite. Even though David had planned to go into battle himself, he was restrained by his men. His parting words to the captains are etched with pity: "Deal gently for my sake with the young man, even with Absalom" (2 Samuel 18:5).

(75) *Why do you think David had such tender feelings for a son who had caused him so much trouble?*

(76) *There in the woods of Ephraim a great slaughter took place that day. What does the term: "the wood devoured more people that day than the sword devoured" mean (2 Samuel 18:8)?*

(77) *Describe the events of Absalom's death (2 Samuel 18:9-18).*

(78) *Why were two messengers sent to tell David of the news and why were their stories conflicting (2 Samuel 18:19-33)?*

This part of the tragedy ends with the famous words: "O my son Absalom! my son, my son Absalom! would God I had died for thee, O Absalom, my son, my son!" (2 Samuel 18:33).

### David Returns To Jerusalem

(2 Samuel 19:1-43) - The triumphant David who skillfully captured the city of the Jebusites and made it the capital of a mighty kingdom was a different David from the physically and emotionally old and broken king who made his way back to Jerusalem. Insurrection within his own house had been eliminated but David was never again a powerful and mighty ruler.

Overtaken in his mourning for Absalom, David could not seem to gain control of himself. It was a wise Joab who realized that the King would lose the loyalty of his supporters with such action. Joab urged David to go out and thank all the supporters.

Evidently David felt a need to be officially escorted back into his kingdom so he called the priests (Zadok and Abiathar) to ask them for this official request.

(79) *Who was made captain of the hosts (2 Samuel 19:13)?*

(80) *The key to regaining the King's place in the hearts of his people is found in 2 Samuel 19:14. What was the reasoning? Does this still work today?*

More than a thousand men met David and his company with a ferryboat at the Jordan River. Among those was Shimei the son of Gera.

(81) *Review 2 Samuel 16:5-8 to refresh your memory concerning Shimei's former actions. Abishai urged death. What was David's reasoning concerning his former enemy (2 Samuel 19:22-23)?*

(82) *How did David receive Mephibosheth (2 Samuel 19:24-30)?*

70

Barzallai the Gileadite, an eighty year old man who had befriended David while he was at Mahanaim and had also given supplies (2 Samuel 17:27-28), helped the King over the Jordan. David wanted to express his appreciation by giving Barzillai a special place of honor in Jerusalem. The elderly man was reluctant to leave his home, however, and requested favor for Chimham. (Some feel that this was the son of Barzillai.)

(83) *Read 1 Kings 2:5-9 to learn of David's deathbed requests concerning some of these men.*

## The Revolt Of Sheba When David Returned To Jerusalem

(2 Samuel 20:1-26) - Before David even reached Jerusalem, another insurrection broke out. The leader was Sheba, a Benjamite, who wanted to destroy the unity by splitting the northern and southern kingdoms.

(84) *In the midst of this narration about Sheba's insurrection the inspired writer interrupts by reporting the fate of David's top concubines who had been left behind in Jerusalem. What happened to them* (2 Samuel 20:3)?

David knew that Sheba's revolt had to be quenched immediately. Summoning Amasa to assemble the soldiers, David became perplexed when the leader failed to fulfill his responsibilities quickly. Instead, the King sent Abishai to take care of the matter. (Joab and Abishai were brothers and hence cousins to Amasa.)

(85) *Relate the manner in which Joab killed Amasa* (2 Samuel 20:8-13).

(86) *When Sheba got to Abel, a town in northern Palestine, the counsel of a wise woman saved the entire town from destruction. What was the compromise* (2 Samuel 20:15-22)?

(87) *List David's officers during the latter years of his life* (2 Samuel 20:23-26).

## The Avenging Of The Gibeonites

(2 Samuel 21:1-14) - Tucked unobtrusively among the pages of inspiration is found one of the most touching stories recorded in the Scriptures.

After David was once again established on his throne in Jerusalem, there was a famine in the land for three years! One can imagine the distress which this condition produced. When the King inquired of

71

Jehovah, the former was told that the situation existed because Saul had killed the Gibeonites, a remnant of the Amorites.

(88) *Read Joshua 9:1-27 to learn why this was a breach of promise.*
(89) *What did the Gibeonites desire for revenge* (2 Samuel 21:3-6)?
(90) *Who was spared* (2 Samuel 21:7)? *Who was offered as an appeasement* (verse 8)? *How do you reconcile 2 Samuel 21:8 with 2 Samuel 6:23? Also examine 1 Samuel 18:19 to learn whose husband Adriel was. Do you think it could have been possible that Michal had been married to Adriel after her sister's death and could have reared his children?*

The seven men were hanged on a hill by the Gibeonites in the days of the harvest (the latter part of April) and their bodies were left there until the beginning of the barley harvest (October). (Note that this was in direct violation of Deuteronomy 21:22,23.) For approximately six months Rizpah, the concubine of Saul, kept a lonely vigil on that hillside not only for her own two sons but also for the sons of Michal. During the day she kept the birds from pecking their rotten bodies. By night she bravely guarded the fleshly remains from the ravages of the wild beasts. Try to step into her shoes and imagine such a pitiful sight. Together with the bones of Saul and Jonathan, David gave all the men a decent burial. After this, the long drought ended.

### David's Last Battle With The Philistines

(2 Samuel 21:15-22) - Once again the Philistines plagued the Israelites and had to be put in their proper place. David went with his men, but his age was sapping his strength and he "waxed faint." Had it not been for the intercession of Abishai, the son of Zeruiah, the King would have been killed by a Philistine giant. From this time on, the soldiers thought it best that their aging leader not engage in physical combat. In another battle with the Philistines four more giants were slain.

### David's Song Of Deliverance

(2 Samuel 22:1-51) - Interspersed in the midst of the account of David's last days is a song of deliverance: " . . . in the day that the Lord had delivered him out of the hand of all his enemies, and out of the hand of Saul." Evidently it was not written at this time.

(91) *The reader would be richly rewarded by carefully reading this song of deliverance and comparing it with Psalm 18.*

## David's Mighty Men

(2 Samuel 23:8-39) - As David neared the end of his days on this earth, the inspired writer deemed it important to enumerate thirty-seven of the most important men in his life.

*(92) Scan through these verses and make a list of the ones whose actions you can recall.*

## David's Numbering Of The People

(2 Samuel 24:1-25) - Against the protests of David's servant Joab, a census of the people was ordered. Usually a census in the East was unpopular because the rationale was either for the purposes of taxation or military conscription. In nine months and twenty days, the people were numbered from Dan to Beersheba on both sides of the Jordan with a final count of approximately eight hundred thousand fighting men in Israel and five hundred thousand in Judah.

After the census David's conscience bothered him, for he knew that this action was not pleasing in God's sight. The prophet God confirmed the King's sense of wrongdoing and gave him a choice of three punishments.

*(93) What were the alternatives (2 Samuel 24:12-14)? Which did David choose (verse 15)? How many people died (verse 15)? How can you account for the deaths of so many innocent people?*

When the messenger of the Lord was at the threshing floor of Araunah, his hand was stayed and the plague was thus ended. Gad instructed the King to erect an altar at this site. Since the threshing floor belonged to Araunah, David negotiated with the owner in an attempt to buy the land. Araunah wanted to give not only the threshing floor but also oxen for sacrifices. David's words of wisdom have echoed through the ages: "Neither will I offer burnt offerings unto the Lord my God of that which doth cost me nothing."

*(94) Apply these words which were spoken hundreds of years ago to today's problems.*

David built the altar, offered the necessary sacrifice, and the plague was stayed. 1 Chronicles 21:26 states that God answered by fire upon the altar. (Araunah's threshing floor later became the site of Solomon's Temple. Although David was denied the privileges of building a dwelling place for Jehovah, this beloved king at least had the satisfaction of providing the location.)

## Abishag Ministers To The King

(1 Kings 1:1-4)-David, the fearless shepherd lad who defied Goliath - David, the brave youth who darted in and out of the hillsides for ten years as King Saul chased his challenge to the throne - David, the ambitious young ruler who united the two divisions of the kingdom and then made Israel a country of considerable power. It was this David who finally succumbed to the natural process of physical decline. At the age of seventy, David was an old man. Any visitor to Israel during the rainy winter season knows the bone chilling climate. The King was cold and could not be warmed. In order to rectify the situation, a fair young virgin by the name of Abishag, a Shunammite, was brought to the King to sleep with him and warm his body; but David did not know her sexually.

## Adonijah's Efforts To Usurp the Throne

(1 Kings 1:5-53) - Perhaps it was the deteriorating condition of David which prompted the desire to select a new ruler. Since there had been no precedent for succession to the throne of Israel, Adonijah, David's oldest surviving son, seemed to be a logical selection to many. Among his supporters were Joab, David's general, and the priest Abiathar. There were other influential people in the court, however, who had different ideas. Benaiah, commander of David's personal bodyguard, was against Adonijah. Nathan, the prophet who had both praised and condemned David through the years, felt that this successor was not the one. Zadok the priest joined the ranks of the opposition. As Adonijah made preparations to have himself declared king, Nathan approached Bathsheba, the mother of Solomon, and warned her of the impending danger. (If Adonijah were made king, he would have the power to have both Solomon and Bathsheba killed.)

Bathsheba, the irresistible woman who was instrumental in one of David's greatest sins, had also now grown old. It was Abishag who ministered to David at this time, but Bathsheba evidently had always had a special place in the King's heart. When she approached the aging ruler, he listened to her plea.

(95) *Upon what basis did Bathsheba claim the throne for her son Solomon* (1 Kings 1:15-21)?

(96) *What news did Nathan relay to David* (1 Kings 1:22-27)?

After reassuring Bathsheba that Solomon would rule, David called for Zadok the priest, Nathan the prophet, and Benaiah the commander of David's personal bodyguard. The King ordered that

Solomon be brought to Gihon on David's own mule. This was only a short distance north of the place where Adonijah's supporters were assembled. The valley of Kidron has a curve at this point. Although the two groups could not see one another, they could each hear the happenings of the other side. After Zadok the priest had anointed Solomon with a horn of oil out of the tabernacle, a trumpet was blown and the people said, "God save King Solomon." Much loud rejoicing followed.

Just around the bend Adonijah's followers were bewildered. It was Jonathan, the son of Abiathar the priest, who informed them of the latest happenings. When they all fled, Adonijah sought refuge on the horns of the altar in the tabernacle in an effort to escape the wrath of Solomon and save his own life. Temporary safety was offered when Solomon promised that his half brother would not be harmed as long as "he will show himself a worthy man" (1 Kings 1:52).

(97) *What incident later prompted the death of Adonijah* (1 Kings 2:13-25)?

### David's Death

(2 Kings 2:1-11) - David had grown very old and feeble, but he had lived long enough to see his desired successor ascend the throne. His wise son Solomon would see the borders of the kingdom enlarged even more and would also see the magnificent temple built. (Note 1 Chronicles 22-29).

Before David died, he gave Solomon some positive advice and also admonished him to deal with some people who had not been completely loyal and to reward those who had been faithful.

(98) *Make a list of these people and try to remember the important events of their lives* (1 Kings 2:5-9).

Very simply and in a matter of fact manner, the inspired writer closed the chapters of David's life: "So David slept with his fathers, and was buried in the city of David. And the days that David reigned over Israel were forty years: seven years reigned he in Hebron, and thirty and three years reigned in Jerusalem" (verses 10 and 11).

### Conclusion

As one ponders the exciting and varied events of David's life, the depth is almost overpowering. God's anointed shepherd lad had successfully led the scattered, loose confederation of tribes into a wealthy, powerful nation. David was not perfect. The "blade" years of his life were more flawless than later years. The ten years of running during the "ear" phase were generally faithful to God. The "full corn in the ear" period presented problems as David became more self-sufficient and perhaps lost some of his sense of dependency upon God. Through all this, however, David is the only human to be the recipient of the title of "a man after God's own heart." Although David did wrong many times, his attitude seemed right and he was always willing to admit his mistakes and ask God's forgiveness. In spite of David's shortcomings, his devotion to God was first. *David is the epitome of every one of us with all our strengths and weaknesses.* His triumph gives hope to each child of God today.

Some of the most beautiful lines in the Scriptures are often overlooked, tucked away in the midst of the last words of David. Psalm 143:5 states: "I remember the days of old." One cannot help but connect the days of old with verses 2-4 of 2 Samuel 23. Although David is speaking of the Messiah to come, the words are also applicable of any ruler of God:

He that ruleth over man must be just,
   ruling in the fear of God.
And he shall be as the light of the morning,
   when the sun riseth,
   even a morning without clouds;
   as the tender grass springing out of the earth
   by clear shinings after rain.

David was old. He was dying. The walls of his Jerusalem palace were cold and damp. He had experienced many joys but also numerous heartaches as even his own family turned against him. But somewhere back in the deep reeesses of David's subconscious being, scenes from his early life on those lonely Judean hills when he tenderly cared for his sheep must have flashed across his mind: the freshness of the light of early morning at sunrise - a blue, cloudless sky - drops of rain on tender spring grass. Perhaps David could forget those troublesome latter years as his thoughts transcended the ages. Again he was close to his own Shepherd as he mentally returned to earlier carefree days and once more walked with his God.

# Making The Application

(In view of our study on David's life, how would you use the principles learned in helping to solve these modern problems?)

1. What should you do when you face a seemingly impossible task?
   (Goliath - David's ten years of running - Absalom's rebellion)
2. How should we respond to those who mistreat us?
   (Saul - Eliab - Shimei)
3. What happens when we think we can rely upon our own strength?
   (pride in numbers)
4. Why should we have patience in waiting for God's promise?
   (the time between the first anointing and David's rule over the entire land)
5. How should we perform in doing small, insignificant tasks?
   (learning to use sling, harp - time at Saul's court)
6. What should we do when we face lust and other temptations?
   (Bathsheba)
7. How can we show gratitude for those who have helped us?
   (Jonathan and Mephibosheth - Barzillai)
8. Why is it important to give of ourselves in service to others?
   (David's faithful men -David before Saul)

77

9. What is wrong with pride?
(David's dancing before the ark)
10. What is the importance of storing up spiritual strength?
(David as a boy - in the wilderness)
11. What should be our attitude when God's answer is "No"?
(David's temple)
12. What does real repentance mean?
(Saul had said, "I have sinned." Yet his sins were not forgiven.)
13. What is our part in accepting the responsibility for what happens?
(David took stones and a sling. He also left spies in Jerusalem when he fled.)
14. Why does every human need a close friend?
(Jonathan)
15. What is our responsibility in caring for our parents?
(David took his parents to Moab.)
16. Why should we look for the good in others?
(David's outlaw followers)
17. Even though sin is forgiven, it carries with it its own consequences, including the hurting of innocent ones.
(death of son of David and Bathsheba - insurrection among other sons - victim of lying and deceit)
18. We must personally pay for whatever we offer God.
(threshing floor of Araunah)
19. Can a faithful child of God have children who go astray? Why?
(Amnon - Absalom)
20. Why should unruly children be punished?
21. What are some evil consequences of polygamy?
22. Prosperity and idleness can lead to ruin.
23. Others:

# Comparison Of David The Shepherd With Christ The Shepherd

**David**                              **Christ**

# Psalm Twenty-Three

*I. Acknowledgement Of Ownership*
  A. The Lord is my shepherd
  B. I shall not want

*II. First The Blade*
  A. He maketh me to lie down in green pastures
  B. He leadeth me beside the still waters
  C. He restoreth my soul
  D. He leadeth me in the paths of righteousness for his name's sake

*III. Then The Ear*
  A. Yea, though I walk through the valley of the shadow of death
  B. I will fear no evil for thou art with me

*IV. After That The Full Corn In The Ear*
  A. Thou preparest a table before me in the presence of mine enemies: thou anoinest my head with oil
  B. My cup runneth over
  C. Surely goodness and mercy shall follow me all the days of my life
  D. And I will dwell in the house of the Lord forever

# The Twenty-Third Psalm

The Twenty-third Psalm has always been very dear to me. At a young age I learned to recite the words. Later I taught it in children's classes and have glued cotton on the little pictures to be taken home. I have written papers on the meaning of the verses. But I really had no idea what the psalm meant until I once became completely helpless and these words echoed over and over through my subconscious mind. Not until then could I fathom the assurance of the strength that comes from the tender, loving arms of the shepherd.

I make no claim to scholarship. I simply need and enjoy an organized study of God's Word. At the conclusion of a four year study of the life of David, I invested four or five months meditating upon this beloved psalm. The more I thought about the words, the more clearly I began to see an outline of David's life in this Scripture. The reader may draw his own conclusions. I simply offer you the fruit of my study.

## I. Acknowledgement of Ownership

A. **The Lord Is My Shepherd** - Perhaps no other creature is as dependent upon someone for daily care as is a sheep. It is utterly helpless and could not long survive without someone's protection. Not only does the animal require a shepherd. The nature of the shepherd determines to a very great extent the sort of life which the helpless lamb will live. The sheep of a cruel shepherd suffers from wild animal attacks, exposure to the elements, physical injuries, lack of nourishment, and polluted water. Just as it is true today of any profession, there are good shepherds who lovingly sacrifice themselves for the very best care of the sheep and there are also poor ones whose selfishness causes them to neglect their sheep, thus producing much pain, discomfort, and even death to the flock.

The child of God, the poor vulnerable creature whose life depends upon the care and guidance of someone else, can proudly claim: "The *Lord* is *my* shepherd!" David's shepherd was Jehovah. The Christian, however, can point to Christ as his shepherd. "I am the good shepherd, the good shepherd giveth his life for the sheep" (John 10:11). What an assurance this is!

Having spent his early years as a faithful shepherd, David knew the majesty of this statement as he proudly acknowledged that Jehovah was *his* protector, the one who would walk through life with him.

**B. I Shall Not Want** - Because of the knowledge that he had a loving, caring shepherd, David could rest in the assurance that ultimately all his essential needs would be met throughout life. How sad it is when the child of God expects a life free from want and hardship. He will meet many obstacles, but there is the blessed assurance that all his essential needs will eventually be cared for. Such a realization is not possible unless one can see beyond this life to the purpose of our brief sojourn on this earth. The trusting lamb can rest assured that no matter what may happen, ultimately everything will work together for his good. He has nothing to worry about as he obediently surrenders his life to the guiding hand of one who will see that the needs are met.

## II. First The Blade

**A. He Maketh Me To Lie Down In Green Pastures** - Sheep will not lie in green pastures until they are content. If anything bothers or distracts them or if they fear for their own safety, they will not lie down. (Remember how David killed a bear and a lion in order to protect his flock.) Small pests and parasites usually breed great discontent among the flock. A hungry sheep will not lie down. The fact that the shepherd led his flock to green pastures meant that his sheep could have all they wanted to eat. After satisfying their hunger, they would be more inclined to contentedly lie down and rest. The food, in addition to the rest and contentment, produced a strong flock. Thus, the lambs were indirectly *made* to lie down in green pastures because they had been freed of distractions and their basic needs had been met.

A strenuous life lay ahead for David. The physical, emotional, and spiritual drain would be tremendous. During those early years of his boyhood and the teen years, the young lad needed the nutritious, lush green grass for his growth in all areas of his life. The years spent on the lonely Judean hillsides served a purpose. David needed to become strong physically in order to endure the ten year flight which lay ahead. Conflict with Saul would also call for emotional stability. David's spiritual faith would be greatly tested over and over in the coming years.

As the young shepherd cared for his sheep, he had time in which to develop properly - to store needed strength for the troublesome times that would come. The strenuous work was good for his physical development which would be needed as the future king literally ran in and out among the caves and hills of Israel. Absence from turmoil and conflict gave David time in which to become emotionally stable: to know who he was and to develop a balanced sense of values. Most people would have broken under the strain of the ten years of fleeing. Spiritually it must have been easy for David to commune with Jehovah as he sang, read the Scriptures, and prayed to his master.

How desperately David needed this building of his strength! We are no different. We meet problems and fail, largely because we have no foundation - no physical, emotional nor spiritual reserve.

How sad it is that we often refuse to lie down in green pastures. We hurry here and there. We bring upon ourselves much of the conflict in our lives. Quiet times are needed. Meditation upon God, His Word, and the proper values in life is fundamental in the development of a strong Christian. How wonderful it is if this contentment can come naturally because our needs have been met and we are free from fears and annoyances. Sometimes, however, we desire to do great things in the Lord's service but we won't "lie down." Then God's providence may "make" us lie down. Perhaps an illness or some hardship in life will literally knock the props out from under us. Then we have time to read from His Word, to become saturated with its truths and to commune with God in prayer. Whether the contentment comes naturally or is providentially imposed upon us, it is necessary for our proper development.

**B. He Leadeth Me Beside The Still Waters** - Nearly three-fourths of a sheep's weight is composed of fluids. Although the animal seems to thrive in semiarid areas, it still requires a certain amount of liquid.

Sheep are afraid of raging, turbulent waters. Perhaps this may be attributed to their sensitive emotions. The creature becomes frightened when the stream is moving rapidly. Therefore, one of the duties of the shepherd is to lead his flock to clean, quiet, still water. In an arid country such as Palestine David no doubt experienced this responsibility countless numbers of times as he so lovingly cared for his charges.

Many parts of the land had no streams nor quiet pools of pure, clean water. Sometimes the shepherd had to resort to cisterns to supply this most basic of the sheep's needs. At other times he had to dig a small hole with his hands for the water. One of the responsibilities of the shepherd was to prevent the thirsty creatures from drinking from puddles of stagnant, parasite infested, muddy water along the path to cool, quiet, clean water.

David's early years were filled with nourishment. Just as his sheep required green pastures and cool, still water for growth, so did the young lad need to develop to the fullest in preparation for the turbulent years of his middle and latter life. The days spent in solitude on the Judean hillsides were essential. The good shepherd offered the necessary nourishment for a healthy physical, emotional and spiritual life. David accepted what his Master provided and was ready when the need arose.

Christ offers us cool, still water. How sad it is when we rebel and either dehydrate or else drink polluted water. How sad!

And Jesus said unto them, I am the
bread of life: he that cometh to me
shall never hunger; and he that
believeth on me shall never thirst.

John 6:35

C. **He Restoreth My Soul** - The term "soul" (*nephesh* in Hebrew) may pose a question to some students at this point. Generally speaking the word soul implies the immortal part of man. Frequently, however, it means life -physical life. In this psalm the logical use seems to be the latter.

How well David knew what it meant to restore life to his lambs. A sheep is one of the most vulnerable of all God's creatures. It may

87

stray from the flock either to become lost or to become the target for some predator. David's skill with his sling and rod no doubt killed many wild animals that would have attacked a defenseless lamb on the outskirts of the safety of the flock. It was not uncommon for a sheep to turn on its back and find that it was powerless to get up again by itself. The average person cannot begin to fathom the love and loyalty of a shepherd toward his sheep. He restores or saves the lives of his charges countless times each year. Frequently his own life must be placed in jeopardy in order to protect the flock. How well David understood this phase of the shepherd's work.

During the early years David's own life was in danger many times. Think back over the events of the "blade" years. The young shepherd was certainly endangering his life as he faced Goliath. In Saul's court how closely was he nearly pinned against the wall with a javelin on more than one occasion. The King tried to put David's life in jeopardy when he requested the lives of a hundred Philistines in exchange for the hand of Michal in marriage.

David understood what it meant when he spoke of a shepherd's responsibility for the lives of his flock. How well did he personally know one's dependence upon God for safety while he was yet a young man.

Christians today can never know the peace which passeth understanding until they learn to depend upon God for the very existence of their lives.

D. **He Leadeth Me In The Paths Of Righteousness For His Name's Sake** - A sheep has no sense of direction. Authorities maintain that it cannot see more than fifteen yards ahead. If left to their own whims, the animals will follow the same paths until they become ruts. All the grass will be destroyed and the sheep will consequently die.

A good shepherd does not drive. He leads his flock. He climbs the same hills with them. He realizes that his charges cannot survive unless he keeps them on the move and shifts them to greener pastures. Some shepherds are lazy. They do not lead their flocks to better land. The good shepherd, however, knows the importance of leading his sheep and constantly keeping them on the move. His name's sake, or reputation, depends upon this. David had led his flock all over the Judean hillsides.

After Jehovah had selected David to one day become the leader of His people, it was necessary that He lead the young man in the right paths in order that he might be ready for the tremendous responsibilities which would eventually be his. At first God led David along the paths of the hillsides of Judah where the young shepherd daily grew physically, emotionally, and spiritually. Such paths alone, however, would not have produced the man needed to lead a nation. Divine providence guided David to the Valley of Elah and the confrontation with Goliath to prove the young man's bravery and place him in a favorable position in the eyes of the people. Jehovah also led David in the paths of Saul's court where he gained knowledge of Israel's government and its problems.

God led. David obediently followed.

The Good Shepherd providentially seeks to lead Christians in the right paths. But "all we like sheep have gone astray; we have turned every one to his own way" (Isaiah 53:6). We often stubbornly rebel, thinking our paths are best; but how often is our judgment faulty. "There is a way which seemeth right unto a man but the end thereof are the ways of death" (Proverbs 14:12 and 16:25).

Patiently He pleads again and again: "I am
the way . . . " (John 14:6). But we do not
always follow. Sometimes our stubbornness
must be broken before we will submit.

## III. Then The Ear

A. **Yea, Though I Walk Through The Valley Of
The Shadow Of Death** - The life of the flock
was not confined to green, gently rolling
meadows. As the shepherd led his sheep to the
best pastures, the paths would sometimes be
perilous. Parts of Israel have rugged mountains
with deep ravines and gulches. It would be extremely difficult for the dependent sheep to
ever cross such land without the careful
guidance of a protective shepherd. No doubt
David's bravery had been displayed under
similar circumstances. (Note that "shadow of
death" is the literal meaning of the Hebrew
word *salmawet*. It occurs twenty times in the
Old Testament. Sometimes the word means
death. In other passages it means other crises
besides death. "Darkness" is the general con-
notation.)

During the second phase of David's life, the
youth most certainly faced death and the
shadow of death many times as he was hunted
as a partridge in the mountains. Each night as
he lay his exhausted body down for a few hours
of much needed rest, David must have known
that danger was always imminent. Saul and his
men could be encamped on the other side of the
mountain. As Jesse's son opened his eyes to the
rays of the sun each morning, there must have
been the ever present realization that he might
meet the King face to face before the evening
shadows would fall. There was constant ten-
sion. The danger was always there. David lived
in the shadow of death for ten years!

B. **I Will Fear No Evil: For Thou Art With Me** - At
this point in the psalm the Shepherd ceases to

be referred to as *He* and is called *Thou*. No longer is Jehovah an abstract being. Now He is the fugitive's friend. The relationship becomes more personal. We cannot face hardships (death as well as many others) with an impersonal deity. God must become a reality - a personal friend - to each of us.

IV. **After That The Full Corn In The Ear**

A. **Thou Preparest A Table Before Me In The Presence Of Mine Enemies: Thou Anointest My Head With Oil** -Scholars differ drastically on this last part of the psalm. Some maintain that it is a continuation of the allegory of the sheep. The table spoken of in verse five is supposed to represent the high tableland to which sheep are driven during the hot months each year. The shepherd's duty is to clear the land, or rid it of poisonous plants which could kill a flock.

A completely different viewpoint is that the allegory shifts from that of sheep and a shepherd to one in which a feast is provided by a host. In the eastern world a banquet for the victor in the very presence of his enemies is a victory celebration.

Frankly, I find that the last interpretation seems to be the most logical one. Here the relationship shifts from a dependent animal trustingly following its master through perilous days to that of a man who has triumphed after much struggle and is rewarded by his host with a celebration feast in the very presence of his enemies. The anointing of the man's head with oil follows the eastern custom of setting one apart in an honored position.

David had experienced many difficult years as he ran from the wrath of Saul. He truly had passed through a valley with the darkest of shadows. His faithfulness is now to be rewarded by a victory celebration in the very presence

91

of his enemies. David had been anointed three times. The first one by Samuel was very limited in its scope. The second one occurred when David was proclaimed king over Judah. The real victory, however, was not apparent until he was anointed by Israel also. These were the enemies who had opposed him for so many years. Now David had reaped the reward for all his years of faithfulness. The victory was complete. Even his enemies had to acknowledge him as king.

The faithful Christian will also receive the ultimate reward if he remains true to the Master throughout life.

B. **My Cup Runneth Over** - When David became the ruler, the kingdom expanded as it had never done before to become the most powerful nation during that period of time. Land, riches, and all sorts of material blessings were given to him. Truly, the blessings in his cup overflowed. Granted, David's latter years were marred by trouble, but most of these adverse circumstances were brought about by his own sins. God had not been slack in fulfilling His promises.

If the Christian will only trust God, an overflowing cup has been promised as the reward.

C. **Surely Goodness And Mercy Shall Follow Me All The Days Of My Life** - David knew that God would be with him. Jehovah had proven His faithfulness through many troublesome times. If God could walk beside the young man when his very life was in danger, David must have felt assurance. Goodness seems to imply kindness. Mercy is rendered "steadfastness" elsewhere. One generally thinks of mercy as unmerited favor. David committed many wrongs during the latter part of his life. Even though he repeatedly sinned, his humble attitude and desire to do right gave him reason to expect mercy and kindness from God.

How sad it is when the Christian cannot find peace by accepting God's goodness, mercy, and grace.

D. **And I Will Dwell In The House Of The Lord Forever** -David had desired to build a magnificent edifice to God, but he was denied the right. The honor was to be given to Solomon. In spite of the denial of a material building, David realized that he would dwell with God forever in a spiritual sense even though he had been denied the right to build the temple as an earthly house for Jehovah.

The faithful child of God has the same assurance that was offered to David. A heavenly home makes the struggle seem worthwhile.

Perhaps no other portion of the Scriptures has been etched in the hearts of Christians as deeply as this one. Not only does it seem to outline the life of David. It has served as a lighthouse for weary followers of God for hundreds of years.

# He Knows The Shepherd

I would like to conclude this study with an old story that is probably already familiar to most of the readers.

Once two men - one old and one young - sat on a platform before an audience. As a part of the program each was to repeat the words of the Twenty-third Psalm. The polished young gentleman, with the eloquence of a silver-tongued orator, started reciting: "The Lord is my shepherd . . . " When he had finished, the listeners loudly applauded his efforts, asking him for an encore.

When it became the turn of the old man, he stepped to the front of the platform as he leaned heavily on his cane. His voice lacked the eloquence of the first speaker. In a feeble, shaking manner, he began repeating the same words: "The Lord is my shepherd . . . "

When he was seated, there was no sound from the listeners - no applause, no cheering for an encore. Instead, a deafening silence permeated the room. After a few minutes, the young man stood to make an explanation.

"Friends, you asked me to come back and repeat the Psalm, but you remained silent when my friend was seated. Do you want to know the difference? I know the Psalm, but he knows the Shepherd!"

# One Night I Had A Dream

I dreamed I was walking along the beach with God, and across the sky flashed scenes from my life. For each scene I noticed two sets of footprints in the sand. One belonged to God and the other belonged to me. When the last scene of my life flashed before me, I looked back and noticed that many times along the path of life there was only one set of footprints. I also noticed that it happened at the very lowest and saddest times in my life.

This really bothered me, and I questioned God about it. "Lord, you said that once I decided to follow you, you would walk with me all the way; but I have noticed that during the troublesome times in my life there was only one set of footprints. I don't understand why, in times when I needed you most, you would leave me."

And God replied, "My precious, precious child, I love you and would never, never leave you during your times of trials and suffering. When you see only one set of footprints, it was then that I carried you."

—Selected

# Bibliography

Clark, Adam. *Clark's Commentary*. Vol. II and III. New York: Abingdon-Cokesbury Press.

Crockett, William Day. *A Harmony of Samuel, Kings and Chronicles*. Grand Rapids, Michigan: Baker Book House, 1975.

DeWelt, Don. *Sacred History and Geography*. Rosemead, California: Old Paths Book Club, 1955.

*Great People of the Bible and How They Lived*. Pleasantville, New York: The Reader's Digest Association, 1974.

Hastings, James, ed. *The Speaker's Bible*. Vol. III. Grand Rapids, Michigan: Baker Book House, 1971.

Jorden, Paul J. *A Man's Man Called by God*. Wheaton, Illinois: SP Publications, Inc., 1980.

Keller, Phillip. *A Shepherd Looks at Psalm 23*. Grand Rapids, Michigan: Zondervan Publishing House, 1970.

Keller, Werner. *The Bible as History*. New York: William Morrow and Company, 1964.

Klinck, Arthur W. *Old Testament History*. Saint Louis, Missouri: Concordia Publishing House, 1958.

Meyer, F.B. *David: Shepherd, Psalmist, King*. Fort Washington, Pennsylvania: Christian Literature Crusade, 1973.

Pfeiffer, Charles. *Ancient Israel from Patriarchal to Roman Times*. Grand Rapids, Michigan: Baker Book House, 1965.

Pfeiffer, Charles, *Baker's Pocket Atlas of the Bible*. Grand Rapids, Michigan: Baker Book House, 1973.

Pfeiffer, Charles. *Jerusalem through the Ages*. Grand Rapids, Michigan: Baker Book House, 1967.

Pink, Arthur. *The Life of David*. Vol. I and II. Swengel, Pennsylvania: Reiner Publications, 1977.

Redpath, Alan. *The Making of a Man of God*. Fleming H. Revel Company, 1962.

Weidenschilling, J.M. *The History of Israel from Moses to Christ*. Saint Louis, Missouri: Concordia Publishing House, 1951.